Table of Cont

Multiplication: A Shortcut for Addition

Multiplication is a shortcut for addition.

Nine softball players are warming up on the field. How many feet are warming up on the field?

$$\begin{array}{r} 2 \\ 2 \\ 2 \\ 2 \\ 2 \\ 2 \\ 2 \\ 2 \\ +2 \\ \hline \end{array}$$

____ feet

2, 4, 6, 8, 10, 12, 14, ____, ____

9 groups of 2 = ____

9 times 2 = ____

$9 \times 2 =$ ____

Multiplication means putting groups of equal size together. Multiplication is a shortcut for addition.

Write each problem as an addition fact and as a multiplication fact.

1. Mario bought 4 baseball cards. Each card cost 5¢. How much did Mario spend?

Addition Fact:

____

Multiplication Fact: __________

2. There are 6 friends watching a movie. How many eyes are watching the movie?

Addition Fact:

____

Multiplication Fact: __________

3. There are 7 friends listening to a band concert. How many ears are listening to the concert?

Addition Fact:

____

Multiplication Fact: __________

4. A stick of gum costs 2¢. How much will 8 sticks of gum cost?

Addition Fact:

____

Multiplication Fact: __________

Solve.

5. $4 \times 2 =$ ____ $6 \times 2 =$ ____ $5 \times 2 =$ ____ $7 \times 2 =$ ____ $3 \times 2 =$ ____

6. $9 \times 2 =$ ____ $1 \times 2 =$ ____ $8 \times 2 =$ ____ $2 \times 2 =$ ____ $10 \times 2 =$ ____

7. **What does multiplication mean?**

Multiplication on a Number Line

Multiplication can be modeled with cubes on a number line.

When you count by 5, you only say every fifth number.

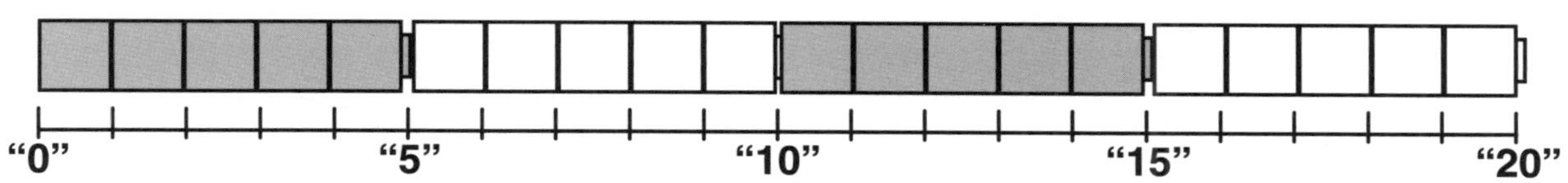

Four skip counts of 5 = ... 5 ...10 ...15 ...20 = **20**

The numbers you say when you count by 5 are called multiples of 5. A **multiple** is the product of a number and a counting number, such as 1, 2, 3, and so on.

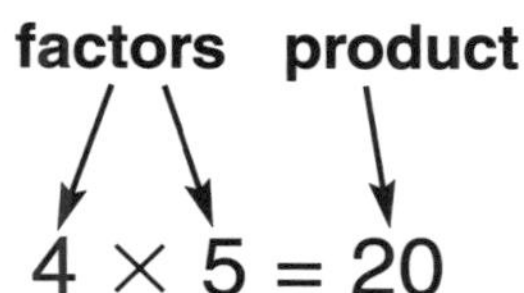

$4 \times 5 = 20$

Count by five. Fill in the missing numbers on the number line below.

1. 0 ___ 10 ___ ___ 25 ___ 35 ___ ___ 50

2. Write an addition fact and a multiplication fact for the pictures.

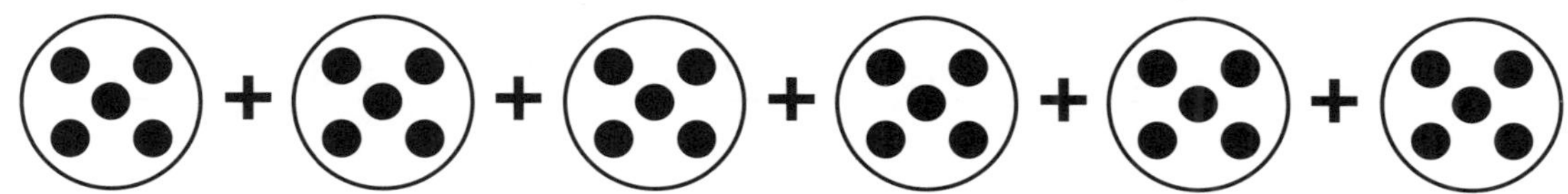

Addition Fact: ______________________

Multiplication Fact: ______________________

Solve.

3. 3×5 5×5 2×5 7×5 4×5 6×5 9×5 8×5

4. $4 \times 5 =$ _____ $7 \times 5 =$ _____ $6 \times 5 =$ _____ $8 \times 5 =$ _____

5. Franco has 6 nickels. He wants to buy a soda that costs 25¢. How much money does Franco have? ______ Does he have enough to buy a soda? ______

6. Victoria has 9 nickels. Hugo has 5 dimes. Who has more money? __________ How much more? __________

The multiples of 2 and 5 have interesting patterns.

7. The multiples of 5 always end in ______ or ______ .

8. The multiples of 2 always end in ____, ____, ____, ____, or 8. They are called _________ numbers.

Multiplying by 0 and 1

The numbers 0 and 1 have special properties in multiplication.

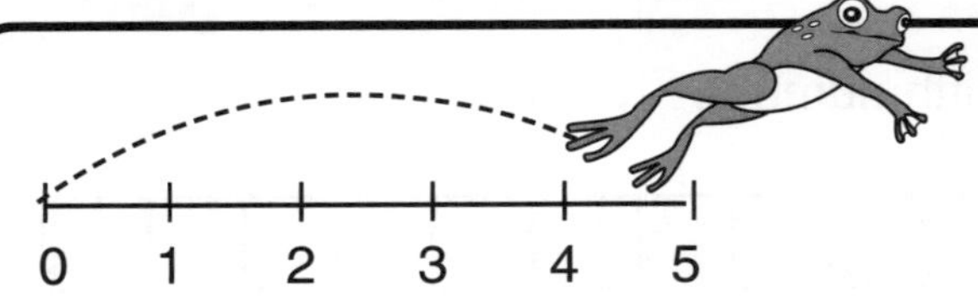

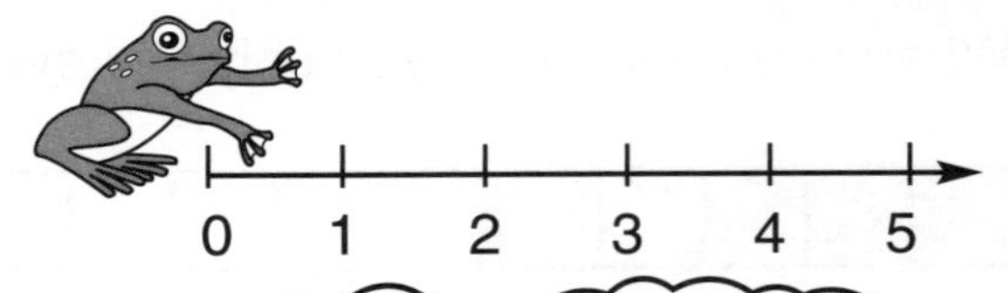

O jumps of any number means you can not move on the number line.

1 jump of 5 = ______

1 × 5 = ______

5 jumps of 1 = ______

5 × 1 = ______

Any number multiplied by 1 equals ____________.

0 jumps of 5 = ______

0 × 5 = ______

Any number multiplied by 0 equals __________.

Find the products.

1.	4 × 1	1 × 7	1 × 2	6 × 1	1 × 1	1 × 5	1 × 8	3 × 1
2.	5 × 0	8 × 0	0 × 6	0 × 2	0 × 7	3 × 0	9 × 0	1 × 4
3.	2 × 1	0 × 8	0 × 9	5 × 1	2 × 0	6 × 0	7 × 1	0 × 3

4. 5 × 0 = _____ 1 × 6 = _____ 4 × _____ = 0 6 × _____ = 6

5. 6 × 2 = _____ 1 × 7 = _____ 2 × 8 = _____ 0 × 8 = _____

6. 8 × 5 = _____ 6 × 0 = _____ 5 × 9 = _____ 9 × 1 = _____

TEST PREP

What number goes in the box to make a true sentence?

5 × ☐ = 0

A 0
B 1
C 5
D 10

Ⓐ Ⓑ Ⓒ Ⓓ

Multiplication as Arrays

An array shows objects in rows and columns.

There are 3 cans of orange juice in a pack. How many cans are in 5 packs?

5 × 3 = ☐

You can draw an array to solve the problem. Make an array to show 5 rows of 3.

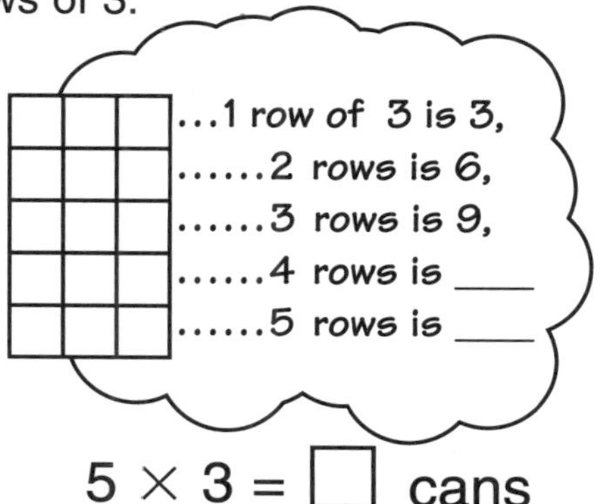

5 × 3 = ☐ cans

Skip count by 3 from 3 to 30.

1.

×	1	2	3	4	5	6	7	8	9	10
3	3						21			

What multiplication fact is shown?

2. 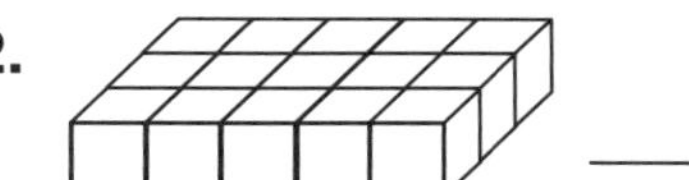 ______________

3. 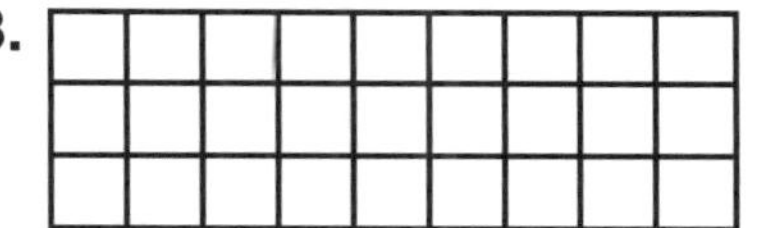 ______________

Solve.

4.

$\begin{array}{r} 5 \\ \times 3 \\ \hline \end{array}$ $\begin{array}{r} 3 \\ \times 3 \\ \hline \end{array}$ $\begin{array}{r} 8 \\ \times 3 \\ \hline \end{array}$ $\begin{array}{r} 6 \\ \times 3 \\ \hline \end{array}$ $\begin{array}{r} 3 \\ \times 9 \\ \hline \end{array}$ $\begin{array}{r} 4 \\ \times 3 \\ \hline \end{array}$ $\begin{array}{r} 3 \\ \times 2 \\ \hline \end{array}$ $\begin{array}{r} 10 \\ \times 3 \\ \hline \end{array}$ $\begin{array}{r} 7 \\ \times 3 \\ \hline \end{array}$

5. 3 × 6 = _____ 8 × 3 = _____ 3 × 9 = _____ 7 × 3 = _____

6. 9 × 3 = _____ 6 × 3 = _____ 3 × 8 = _____ 3 × 7 = _____

7. George sets the table for 8 people. He sets 1 fork, 1 knife, and 1 spoon at each seat. How many forks, knives, and spoons does he put on the table in all?

____

8. Jessie has 4 each of 3 kinds of beads. How many beads does she have in all?

____

9. **You have learned two important ways to draw multiplication facts. Tell how you would draw the multiplication fact 4 × 3.**

Order Property

A tray made of tiles has 4 rows of 6 tiles each. How many tiles are on the tray?

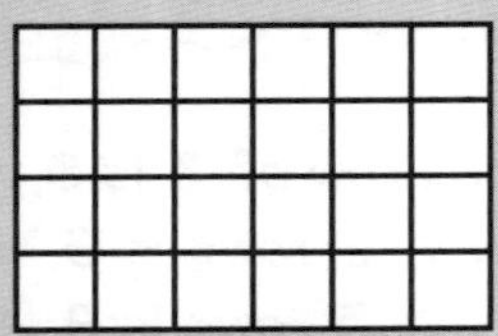

4 × 6 = ☐

The tray is turned. Now there are 6 rows of 4 tiles. How many tiles are on the tray?

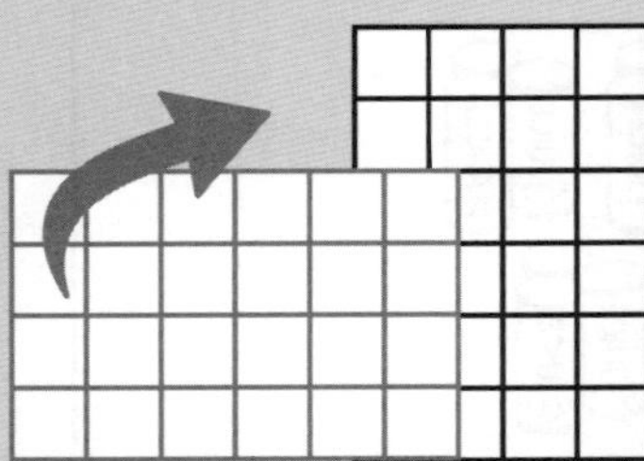

6 × 4 = ☐

How do the answers compare? ______________________________.

The order property:

When you change the order of two factors, the product is ____________________.

Complete the multiplication table.

1.

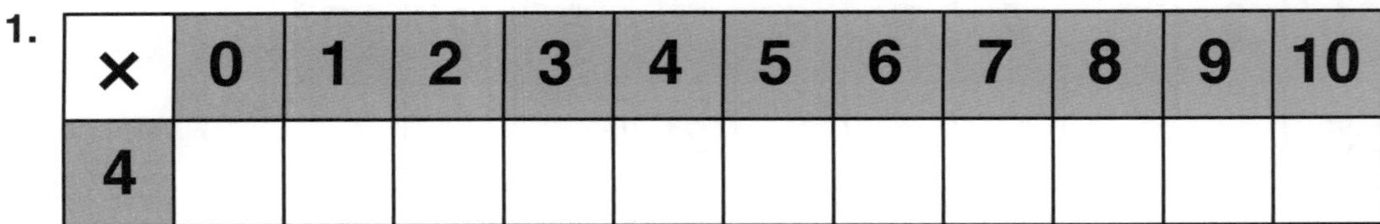

×	0	1	2	3	4	5	6	7	8	9	10
4											

Find the product.

2. 3 × 7 = _____ 7 × 3 = _____

3. 5 × 4 = _____ 4 × 5 = _____

4. 5 × 3 = _____ 3 × 5 = _____

5. 9 × 5 = _____ 5 × 9 = _____

Use the order property. Find the missing number.

6. 2 × 5 = ☐ × 2

7. 4 × 6 = ☐ × 4

8. 3 × 9 = ☐ × 3

9. Jessie has 2 rows of 8 cookies. What is another way to arrange the cookies in equal rows? How many cookies does Jessie have?

____

____

10. George is baking muffins. He has 3 rows of 4 muffins in each row. What is another way to arrange the muffins in rows? How many muffins does George have?

____

____

Explain the order property of multiplication. Use words and draw a picture of an array to demonstrate. Why is it helpful to know the order property?

Mental Math

Use doubles to find multiples of 2.
2 twos = 4, 2 threes = 6, 2 fours = 8, 2 fives = 10, etc.

1.

×	0	1	2	3	4	5	6	7	8	9	10
2											

Use doubles plus the number to find multiples of 3.
3 × 4 = double 4 plus 4 or 12, 3 × 5 = double 5 plus 5 or 15, etc.

2.

×	0	1	2	3	4	5	6	7	8	9	10
3											

Use double doubles to find multiples of 4.
4 × 3 = double 3 plus double 3 or 12, 4 × 5 = double 5 plus double 5 or 20, etc.

3.

×	0	1	2	3	4	5	6	7	8	9	10
4											

An even number of fives ends in 0: 2 × 5 = 10, 4 × 5 = 20, 6 × 5 = 30, etc.
An odd number of fives ends in 5: 1 × 5 = 5, 3 × 5 = 15, 5 × 5 = 25, etc.

4.

×	0	1	2	3	4	5	6	7	8	9	10
5											

5. There are 3 students who are each raising one hand. How many fingers are raised?

   ____

6. There are 6 tables in the room. There are 4 students at each table. How many total students are there?

   ____

Breaking Apart the Number 6

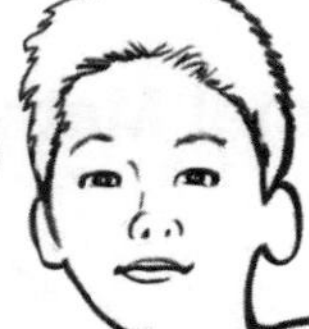

Here are two ways to multiply 6 by 7.

To multiply a number by <u>6</u>, think of <u>3</u> times the number plus <u>3</u> times the number.

$6 \times 7 =$

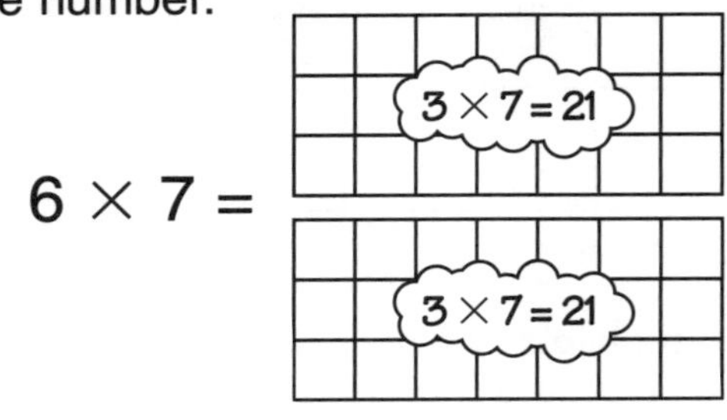

$6 \times 7 =$ ☐

To multiply a number by <u>6</u>, think of <u>5</u> times the number plus <u>the number</u>.

$6 \times 8 =$

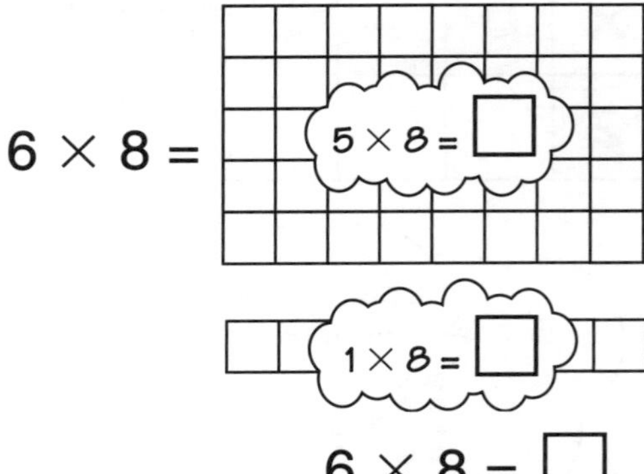

$6 \times 8 =$ ☐

Count by 6. Fill in the missing numbers on the number line below.

1.

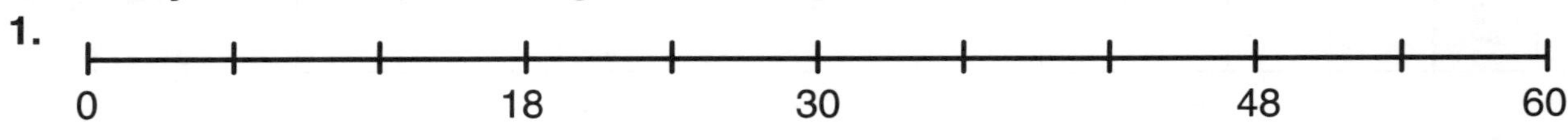

Solve.

2.

5	6	6	9	6	6	3	7
× 6	× 4	× 6	× 6	× 8	× 7	× 6	× 6

3. $8 \times 6 =$ ______ $6 \times 7 =$ ______ $6 \times 6 =$ ______ $6 \times 9 =$ ______

4. If you know that $6 \times 7 = 42$, then you know that $7 \times 6 =$ ☐.

5. If you know the order property and your multiplication facts through 5, there are only 10 new facts to learn. Four of them are with 6.

$6 \times 6 =$ ______ $6 \times 7 =$ ______
$6 \times 8 =$ ______ $6 \times 9 =$ ______

Fill in the answers in the shaded spaces of the multiplication chart.

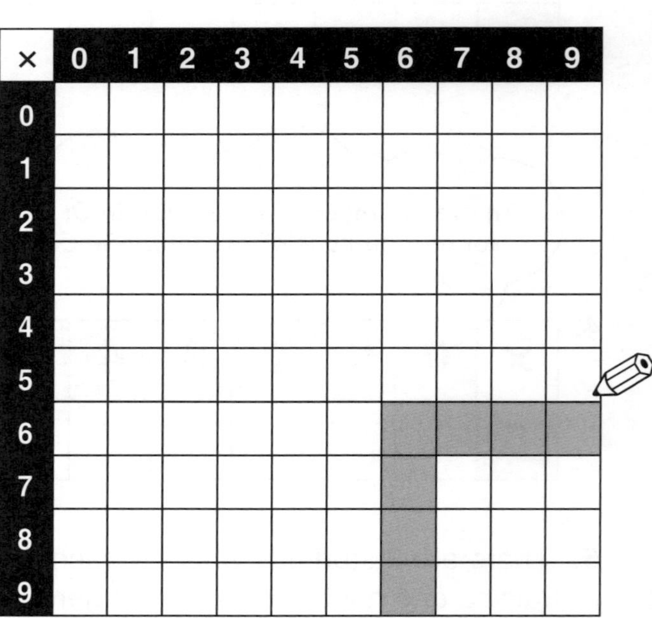

×	0	1	2	3	4	5	6	7	8	9
0										
1										
2										
3										
4										
5										
6										
7										
8										
9										

TEST PREP  $8 \times 6 =$ ☐ **A** 14 **B** 42 **C** 48 **D** 54

Ⓐ Ⓑ Ⓒ Ⓓ

Breaking Apart the Numbers 7 and 8

You can find the multiplication facts for 7 and 8 by breaking the array apart into smaller arrays.

8 groups of 7 =
4 groups of 7 + 4 groups of 7

8 × 7

4 groups of 7 = _____

+

4 groups of 7 = _____

is

8 groups of 7 = ☐

8 × 7 = ☐

9 groups of 8 =
5 groups of 8 + 4 groups of 8

9 × 8

5 groups of 8 = _____

+

4 groups of 8 = _____

is

9 groups of 8 = ☐

9 × 8 = ☐

Draw a thick line to show how to find the product by breaking the larger group apart into two smaller groups. Solve.

1. 7 × 7

5 groups of 7 = ____
2 groups of 7 = ____

7 groups of 7 = ☐

7 × 7 = ☐

2.

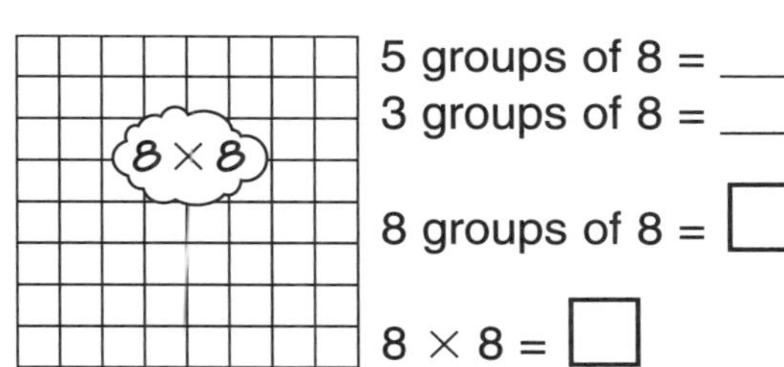

5 groups of 8 = ____
3 groups of 8 = ____

8 groups of 8 = ☐

8 × 8 = ☐

Complete the table of multiples of 7 and 8.

3.

×	0	1	2	3	4	5	6	7	8	9	10
7											
8											

Use the order property to write another fact for the given fact.

4. 8 × 7 = 56 ________________ 9 × 8 = 72 ________________

9 × 7 = 63 ________________ 9 × 6 = 54 ________________

8 × 6 = 48 ________________ 6 × 7 = 42 ________________

Problem Solving: Draw a Picture, Write a Number Sentence

Drawing pictures helps you understand word problems. You can write a number sentence from the picture.

There are 4 children looking out the window. How many eyes are looking out the window?

4 groups × 2 eyes each = ☐ eyes

4 × 2 = ☐ eyes

Draw a picture. Use a box to stand for the unknown number.

1. There are 4 ants.
Each ant has 6 legs.
How many legs in all?

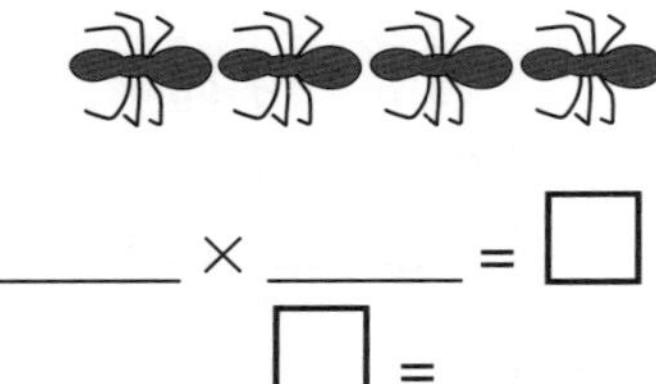

______ × ______ = ☐

☐ = ______

2. There are 2 boxes of crayons, and 8 crayons in each box.
How many crayons in all?

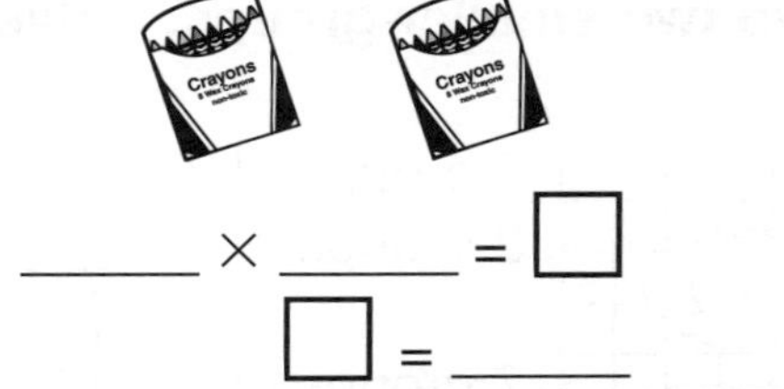

______ × ______ = ☐

☐ = ______

3. There are 5 flowers, and 6 petals on each flower.
How many petals in all?

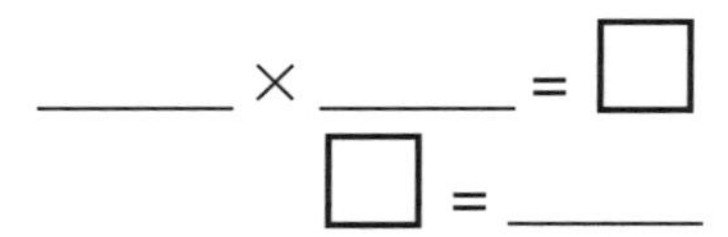

______ × ______ = ☐

☐ = ______

4. There are 3 bags of marbles, and 6 marbles in each bag.
How many marbles in all?

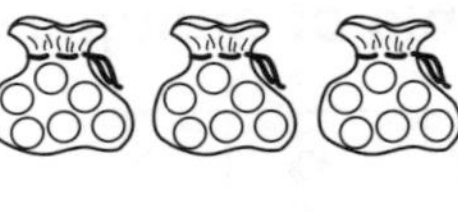

______ × ______ = ☐

☐ = ______

5. There is a pack of gum.
Each pack has 5 sticks of gum.
How many sticks in all?

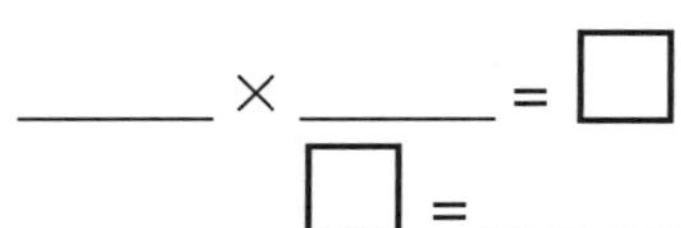

______ × ______ = ☐

☐ = ______

6. There are 3 spiders.
Each spider has 8 legs.
How many legs in all?

______ × ______ = ☐

☐ = ______

n=?

Strategies for Multiplying by 9 and 10

You can find the multiplication facts for 9 on your fingers, or you can use the facts for 10.

Think of numbering your fingers from 1 to 9.

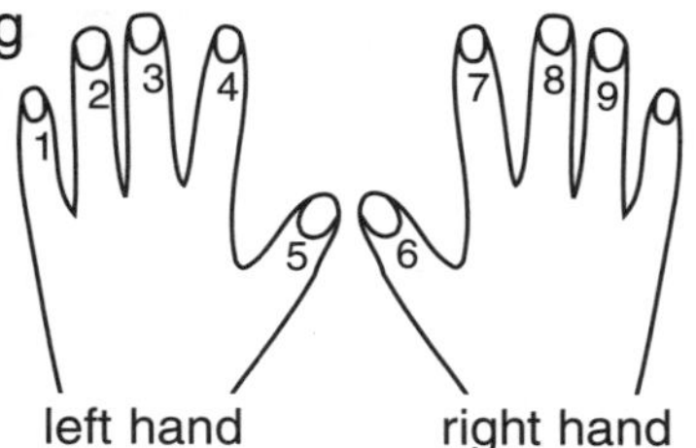

To multiply 4 × 9, hide your "4" finger. There are 3 fingers to the left and 6 fingers to the right.

3 6

4 × 9 = □

To multiply 9 × 7 think of 10 × 7.

Then subtract one 7 from the product.

= 70
− 7

9 x 7 = 63

Try it on 9 × 8.

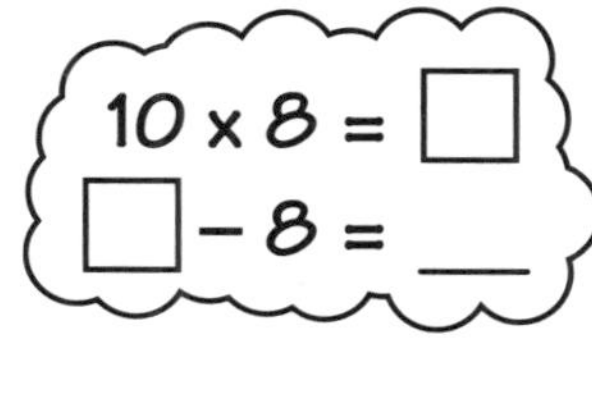

9 × 8 = ____

Complete the multiplication table for 9 and 10.

1.

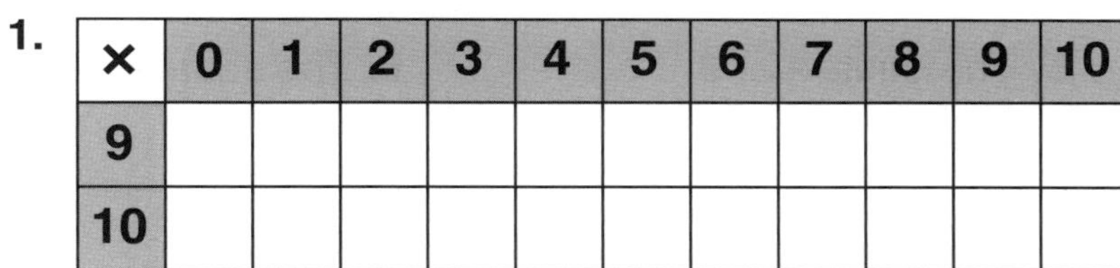

×	0	1	2	3	4	5	6	7	8	9	10
9											
10											

2. Describe the pattern of the sum of the digits for the products of 9. ____________

3. Describe the pattern of the products of 10. ____________

Use your fingers to multiply each number by 9.

4. 9 × 3 = ______ 9 × 6 = ______ 9 × 9 = ______ 9 × 7 = ______

Multiply each number by 10. Subtract one of the numbers from the product.

5. 9 × 6 = (10 × 6 = 60)
− 6 = 54
9 × 6 = □

9 × 8 = (10 × 8 =)
− 8 = ____
9 × 8 = □

9 × 9 = (10 × 9 =)
− 9 = ____
9 × 9 = □

Write <, >, or = in each ◯.

6. 9 × 6 ◯ 5 × 10 **7.** 10 × 4 ◯ 4 × 10 **8.** 9 × 7 ◯ 8 × 10

Square Numbers

The square of a number forms a square array because it is the product of a number multiplied by itself.

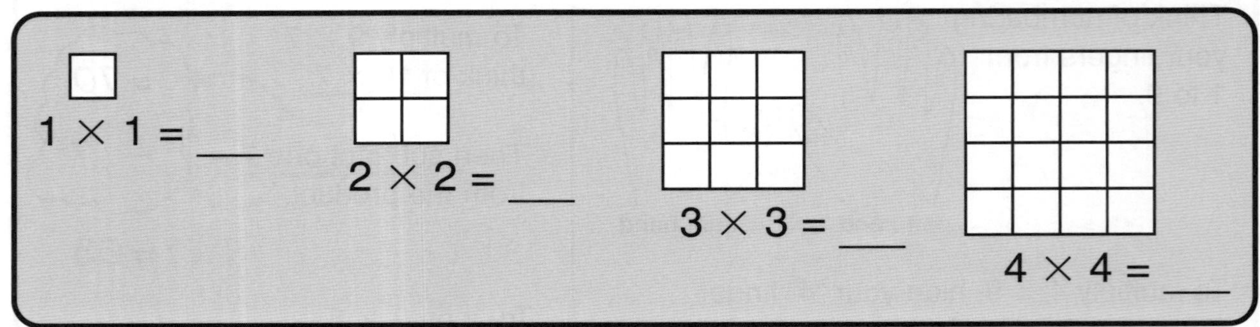

Outline the square array. Write the answer to the multiplication fact below the square.

1. The square of 5

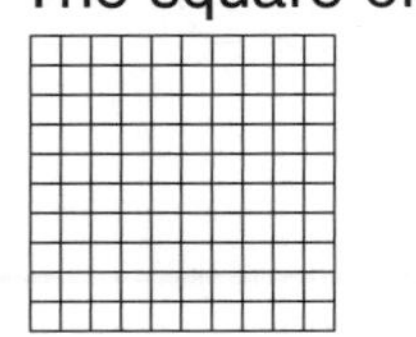

5 × 5 = _____

2. The square of 6

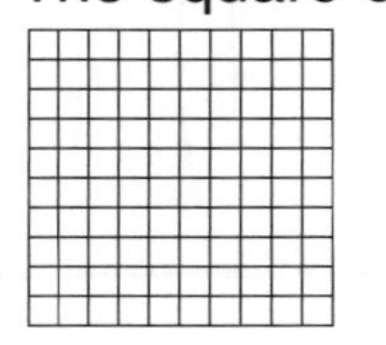

6 × 6 = _____

3. The square of 7

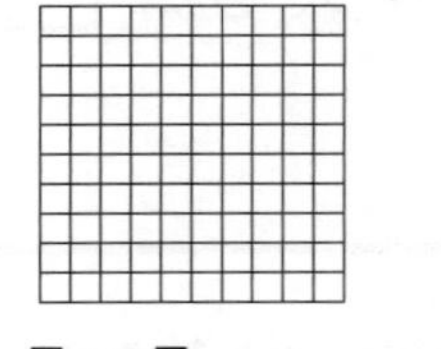

7 × 7 = _____

4. The square of 8

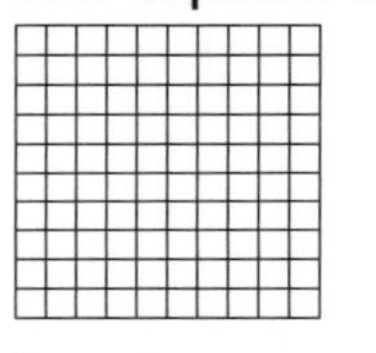

8 × 8 = _____

5. The square of 9

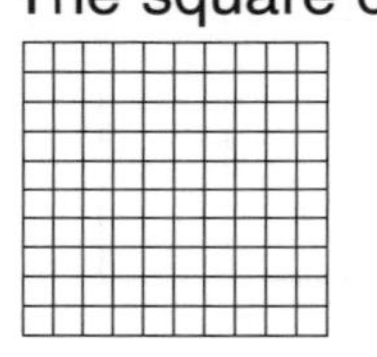

9 × 9 = _____

6. The square of 10

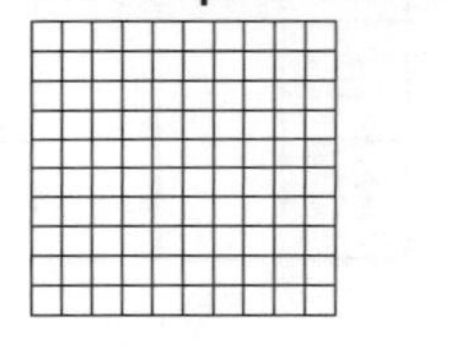

10 × 10 = _____

Write the multiplication fact for each array. Circle yes or no to tell whether the product is the square of a number.

7.

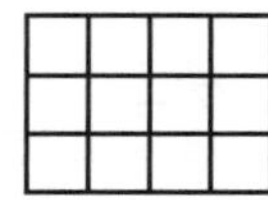

___ × ___ = ___
(yes, no)

8.

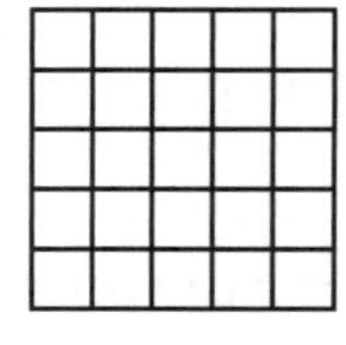

___ × ___ = ___
(yes, no)

9.

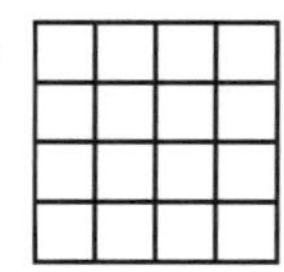

___ × ___ = ___
(yes, no)

10.

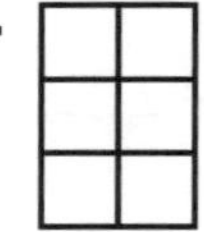

___ × ___ = ___
(yes, no)

11. List the squares of each number from 1 to 10:

______, ______, ______, ______, ______, ______, ______, ______, ______, ______

12. **Why is 64 called a "square number?"**

Completing a Multiplication Table

On a multiplication table, the product is found where the factor **row** and the factor **column** meet. To find the product of 4 $\times$ 6, look where the factor row of 4 meets the factor column of 6 at the number 24. **Use a pencil to complete the table.**

×	0	1	2	3	4	5	6	7	8	9	10
0	0				0						
1							6				
2									16		
3						15					
4							24				
5								35			
6									48		
7					28						
8								56			
9										81	
10						50					

There are many ways to find the product of 2 numbers. You can make groups of equal size, skip count, use a number line, make an array, use the order property, think of doubles, or take apart an array and add the products of the smaller parts together.

Use two different ways to find the product of 4 $\times$ 6. Use words, pictures, and numbers to explain.

Multiplication Patterns: Functions

A **function** is a relationship between two numbers where the quantity of one number depends upon the quantity of the other.

Room 301 planted bean seeds. Each student put 3 seeds in a cup of dirt.

Draw a picture of the number of cups and seeds that 9 students used.

Make a table to show how the number of cups is related to the number of seeds. Find the pattern.

No. of cups	1	2	3	4	5	6	7	8	9
No. of seeds	3								

Pattern: number of seeds = ______________ × the number of ______________ .

Make a table to show the cost of buying up to 9 items at the same price. Find the pattern.

1. A used paperback book costs $2. Find the cost of buying from 1 to 9 books.

No. of books	1	2	3	4	5	6	7	8	9
Total cost	$2								

Pattern: total cost = ______________ × the number of ______________ .

2. Baseballs cost $5 each. Find the cost of buying from 1 to 9 baseballs.

No. of baseballs	1	2	3	4	5	6	7	8	9
Total cost	$5								

Pattern: total cost = ______________ × the number of ______________ .

3. At Replay Music, compact discs cost $4 each. Find the cost of buying from 1 to 9 compact discs.

No. of CDs	1	2	3	4	5	6	7	8	9
Total cost	$4								

Pattern: total cost = ______________ × the number of ______________ .

$n=?$

Function Machine

A function machine follows the same rule or pattern each time a number is put into it. Look for a pattern in the INPUT and OUTPUT numbers of the table below.

You can make a table to find the pattern.

A spider has 8 legs. Rule: spiders × 8 = legs

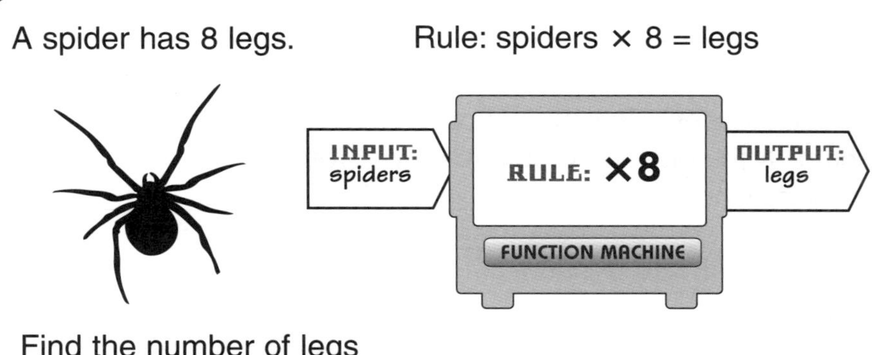

INPUT	OUTPUT
number of spiders	number of legs
1	8
2	
3	
4	

Find the number of legs on 2 spiders, on 3 spiders, and on 4 spiders.

Find the pattern or rule. Use the rule to complete each table.

1. A dog has 4 legs. Find the number of legs on 1, 2, 3, and 4 dogs.

Rule: *dogs × 4 = legs*

Input (dogs)	Output (legs)
1	4
2	
3	
4	

2. An ant has 6 legs. Find the number of legs on 2, 3, and 4 ants.

Rule: ______________________

Input (ants)	Output (legs)
1	6
2	
3	
4	

3. Jake rides his bike about 10 miles in 1 hour. Find how far he travels in 2 hours, 3 hours, and 4 hours.

Rule: ______________________

Input (hours)	Output (miles)
1	10
2	
3	
4	

4. Jake's sister works at a fast food restaurant. She earns $7 each hour. Find how much she earns in 2 hours, 3 hours, and 4 hours.

Rule: ______________________

Input (hours)	Output (dollars)
1	$ 7
2	
3	
4	

TEST PREP

What number goes in the box to complete the pattern?

3	6		12

A 7 Ⓐ
B 8 Ⓑ
C 9 Ⓒ
D 12 Ⓓ

n=?

Multiplying Three Numbers: The Grouping Property

The **grouping property of multiplication** tells us that the order in which you multiply 3 numbers does not change the final product. **Parentheses** indicate which operations are to be done first.

Kim has been taking piano lessons for 3 months. She has 4 lessons each month. She practices 2 hours for each lesson. How many hours does she practice during 3 months? Kim draws picture **A** to solve the problem. Kim's brother draws picture **B** to solve the problem. Who is right? ________ Explain. ________________

____

[A]

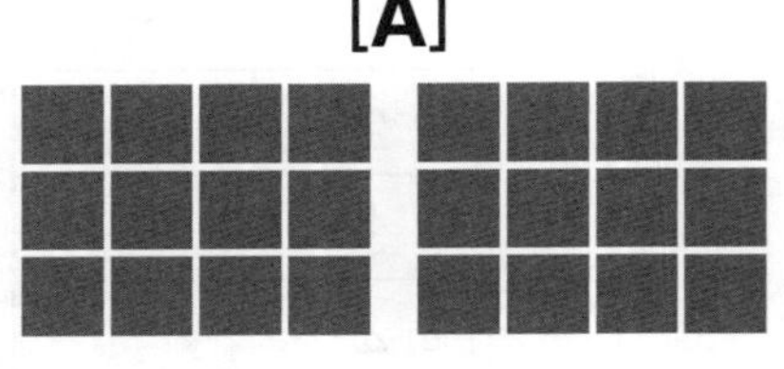

2 groups of 3×4

$2 \times (3 \times 4)$

________ hours of practice

[B]

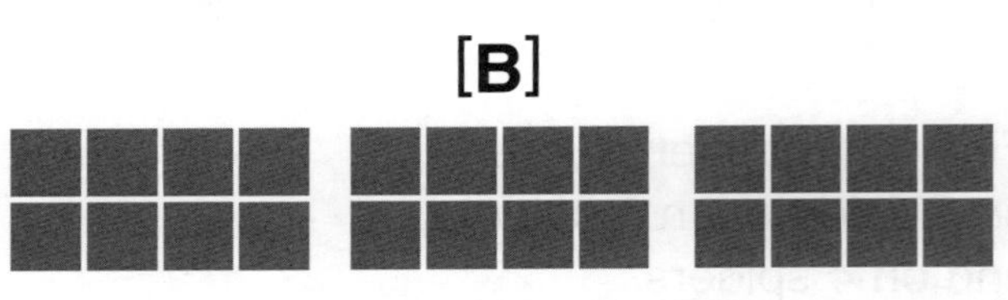

3 groups of 2×4

$3 \times (2 \times 4)$

________ hours of practice

Multiply the three numbers in different ways. Compare the answers.

1. $5 \times (2 \times 4)$ ____ × ____ = ______ $(5 \times 2) \times 4$ ____ × ____ = ______

The answers are ________________.

2. $(4 \times 2) \times 3$ ____ × ____ = ______ $4 \times (2 \times 3)$ ____ × ____ = ______

The answers are ________________.

Find the number that goes in the $\square$.

3. $(2 \times \square) \times 5 = 2 \times (4 \times 5)$

4. $(5 \times 2) \times 3 = 5 \times (\square \times 3)$

5. $3 \times (\square \times 2) = (3 \times 5) \times 2$

6. $(3 \times 2) \times \square = 3 \times (2 \times 5)$

Use mental math to find the products.

7. $(3 \times 2) \times 5 =$ ______

8. $2 \times (2 \times 3) =$ ______

9. $(3 \times 2) \times 4 =$ ______

10. **Describe the grouping property of multiplication in your own words.**

TEST PREP

$(2 \times 3) \times 5 = 2 \times (\square \times 5)$

A 2 Ⓐ
B 3 Ⓑ
C 5 Ⓒ
D 6 Ⓓ

Multiplying Multiples of 10 by a 1-Digit Number

In *Charlie and the Great Glass Elevator*, Grandma Josephine takes 4 pills. Each pill makes her 20 years younger. How much younger is she?

I can build 20 four times.

TENS	ONES

I can add 20 four times...

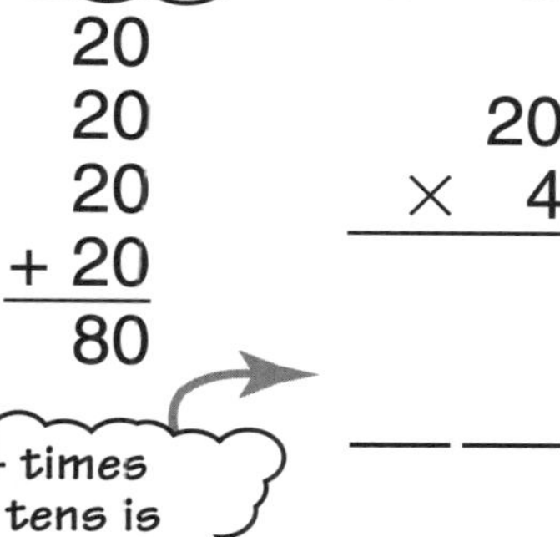

$$\begin{array}{r} 20 \\ 20 \\ 20 \\ +\ 20 \\ \hline 80 \end{array}$$

or I can multiply 20 by 4.

$$\begin{array}{r} 20 \\ \times\ \ 4 \\ \hline \_\ \_ \end{array}$$

4 times 2 tens is 8 tens

4 times 0 ones is 0

She is ______ years younger.

Use base ten blocks to multiply.

1. $\begin{array}{r} 20 \\ \times 4 \\ \hline \end{array}$ $\begin{array}{r} 20 \\ \times 3 \\ \hline \end{array}$ $\begin{array}{r} 20 \\ \times 1 \\ \hline \end{array}$ $\begin{array}{r} 20 \\ \times 2 \\ \hline \end{array}$ $\begin{array}{r} 40 \\ \times 2 \\ \hline \end{array}$ $\begin{array}{r} 30 \\ \times 3 \\ \hline \end{array}$ $\begin{array}{r} 30 \\ \times 2 \\ \hline \end{array}$

Use basic facts and a pattern to multiply multiples of 10.

2. $\begin{array}{r} 30 \\ \times 4 \\ \hline 120 \end{array}$ $\begin{array}{r} 50 \\ \times 3 \\ \hline \end{array}$ $\begin{array}{r} 60 \\ \times 4 \\ \hline \end{array}$ $\begin{array}{r} 30 \\ \times 8 \\ \hline \end{array}$ $\begin{array}{r} 20 \\ \times 6 \\ \hline \end{array}$ $\begin{array}{r} 40 \\ \times 4 \\ \hline \end{array}$ $\begin{array}{r} 70 \\ \times 5 \\ \hline \end{array}$

3. $\begin{array}{r} 20 \\ \times 5 \\ \hline \end{array}$ $\begin{array}{r} 30 \\ \times 6 \\ \hline \end{array}$ $\begin{array}{r} 40 \\ \times 3 \\ \hline \end{array}$ $\begin{array}{r} 50 \\ \times 5 \\ \hline \end{array}$ $\begin{array}{r} 20 \\ \times 7 \\ \hline \end{array}$ $\begin{array}{r} 40 \\ \times 5 \\ \hline \end{array}$ $\begin{array}{r} 50 \\ \times 6 \\ \hline \end{array}$ $\begin{array}{r} 30 \\ \times 7 \\ \hline \end{array}$

Write a number sentence. Solve.

4. Children breathe about 30 times a minute. How many times would a child breathe in 5 minutes?

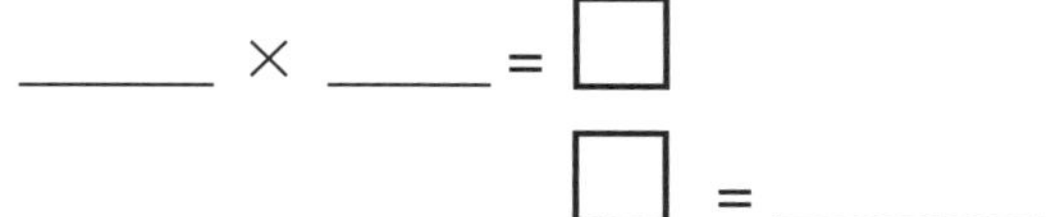

_____ × _____ = ☐

☐ = ________

5. When a brown bear gets ready to hibernate, it eats 40 pounds of plants and berries a night. How much would it eat in 7 nights?

_____ × _____ = ☐

☐ = ________

TEST PREP

6 × 20 = ☐

A 12 Ⓐ
B 26 Ⓑ
C 120 Ⓒ
D 620 Ⓓ

Multiplying a 2-Digit by a 1-Digit Number

1. Read and understand.
2. Find the question and needed facts.
3. Decide on a process.

You can use base ten blocks to find a pattern.

Tom collects baseball cards and stores them in a book. Each page in the book holds 12 cards. How many cards will fill 4 pages?

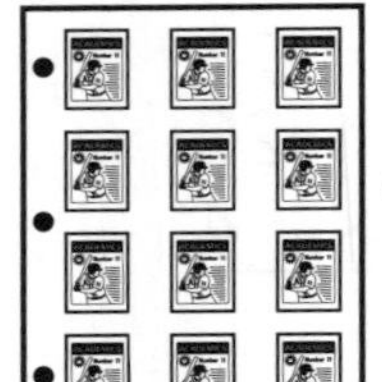

Tom has 12 + 12 + 12 + 12 or 4 groups of 12. This is a multiplication problem: 4 x 12

1. Build 4 sets of 12.
Record the number of tens and ones.

TENS	ONES
4 tens	8 ones

4 tens + 8 ones

40 + 8 = ☐

2. You can use a pattern. Multiply 4 by the value of each digit.

$$\begin{array}{r} 12 \\ \times\ 4 \\ \hline \end{array} \longrightarrow \begin{array}{r} 10 + 2 \\ \times\ \ \ \ 4 \\ \hline \end{array}$$

40 + 8 = ☐

3. You can use a shortcut.

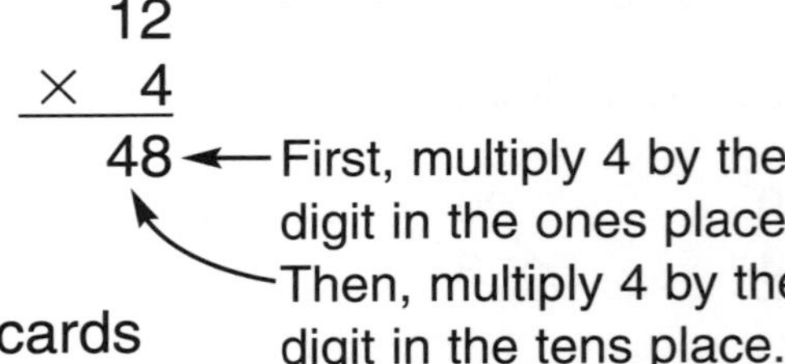

$$\begin{array}{r} 12 \\ \times\ 4 \\ \hline 48 \end{array}$$

First, multiply 4 by the digit in the ones place.
Then, multiply 4 by the digit in the tens place.

_____ cards

1. $\begin{array}{r} 12 \\ \times 2 \\ \hline \end{array}$ ___ tens + ___ ones = ☐

2. $\begin{array}{r} 32 \\ \times 3 \\ \hline \end{array}$ ___ tens + ___ ones = ☐

3. $\begin{array}{r} 22 \\ \times 3 \\ \hline \end{array}$ ___ tens + ___ ones = ☐

Use a pattern. Multiply the value of each digit.

4. $\begin{array}{r} 13 \\ \times 2 \\ \hline \end{array} = \begin{array}{r} 10 + 3 \\ \times\ \ \ 2 \\ \hline \end{array}$ 20 + 6 = ☐

5. $\begin{array}{r} 23 \\ \times 3 \\ \hline \end{array} = \begin{array}{r} 20 + 3 \\ \times\ \ \ 3 \\ \hline \end{array}$ ___ + ___ = ☐

6. $\begin{array}{r} 34 \\ \times 2 \\ \hline \end{array} = \begin{array}{r} 30 + 4 \\ \times\ \ \ 2 \\ \hline \end{array}$ ___ + ___ = ☐

Use a shortcut to multiply.

7. $\begin{array}{r} 14 \\ \times 2 \\ \hline \end{array}$ **8.** $\begin{array}{r} 22 \\ \times 4 \\ \hline \end{array}$ **9.** $\begin{array}{r} 43 \\ \times 2 \\ \hline \end{array}$ **10.** $\begin{array}{r} 33 \\ \times 3 \\ \hline \end{array}$

11. There are 23 students in each of the 2 fourth grade classrooms. How many students are there in fourth grade?

_____

12. Miles Davis Elementary has 2 bands. Each band has 31 members. How many students are there in the bands altogether?

_____

Multiplying Money by a 1-Digit Number

Students can buy healthy snacks at lunch. Fill in the chart that shows the cost of each snack.

HEALTHY SNACKS			
Number	10¢	11¢	12¢
1			
2			
3			

How much do 3 apples cost?

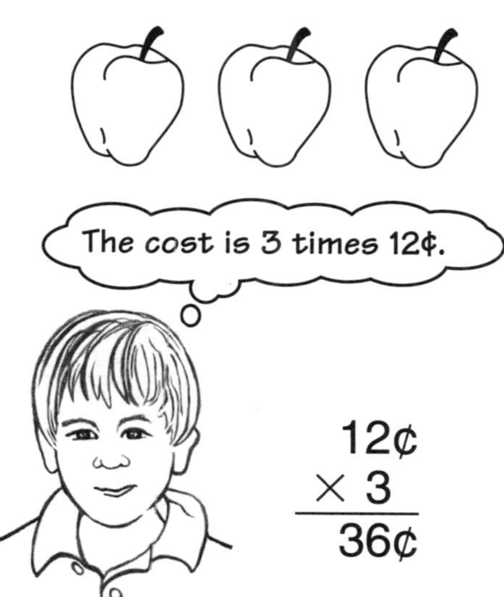

$$\begin{array}{r} 12¢ \\ \times\ 3 \\ \hline 36¢ \end{array}$$

Use the chart above to solve.

1. How much will 4 apples cost? ________

2. How much will 4 bags of nuts cost? ________

Find the products.

3. $\begin{array}{r} 30¢ \\ \times\ 3 \\ \hline \end{array}$

4. $\begin{array}{r} 24¢ \\ \times\ 2 \\ \hline \end{array}$

5. $\begin{array}{r} 23¢ \\ \times\ 3 \\ \hline \end{array}$

6. $\begin{array}{r} 43¢ \\ \times\ 2 \\ \hline \end{array}$

7. $\begin{array}{r} \$\ 20 \\ \times\ 3 \\ \hline \end{array}$

8. $\begin{array}{r} \$\ 21 \\ \times\ 4 \\ \hline \end{array}$

9. $\begin{array}{r} \$\ 32 \\ \times\ 3 \\ \hline \end{array}$

10. $\begin{array}{r} \$\ 34 \\ \times\ 2 \\ \hline \end{array}$

11. Jovita bought 3 cans of soda for 32¢ each. How much did she spend? ________

12. Snack crackers cost 14¢ each. How much will 2 snack crackers cost? ________

TEST PREP 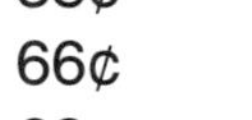

Choose the correct answer.

$\begin{array}{r} 34¢ \\ \times\ 2 \\ \hline \end{array}$

A 36¢
B 38¢
C 66¢
D 68¢

Ⓐ Ⓑ Ⓒ Ⓓ

Multiplication with Regrouping

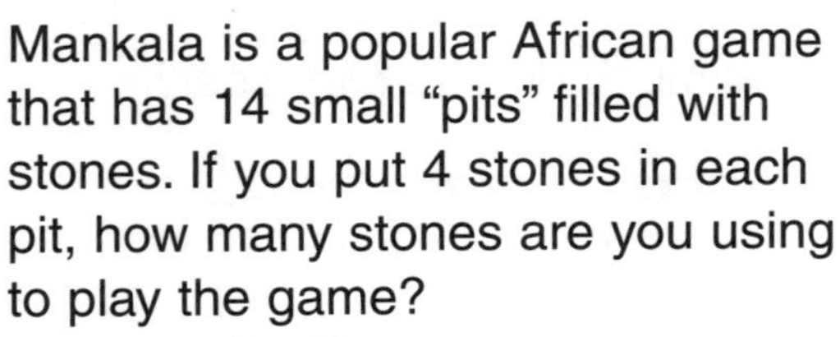

Mankala is a popular African game that has 14 small "pits" filled with stones. If you put 4 stones in each pit, how many stones are you using to play the game?

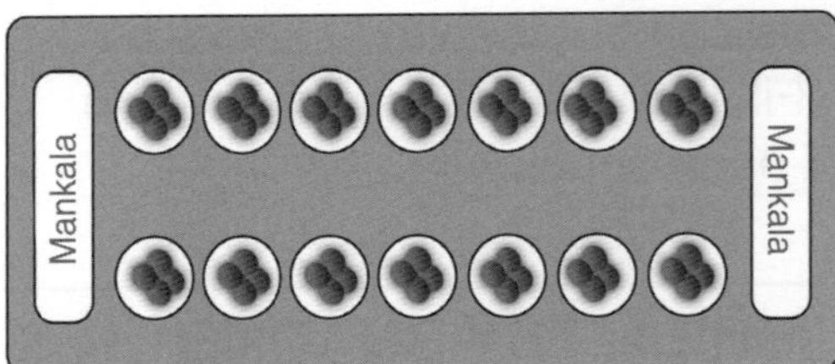

14 pits ... 4 stones in each pit. First, build 14 four times.

Tens	Ones

4 tens 16 ones

Now I can change 10 ones for 1 ten.

Tens	Ones

5 tens 6 ones = 56

I can write it this way.

$$\begin{array}{r} {}^{1}14 \\ \times\ 4 \\ \hline 56 \end{array}$$

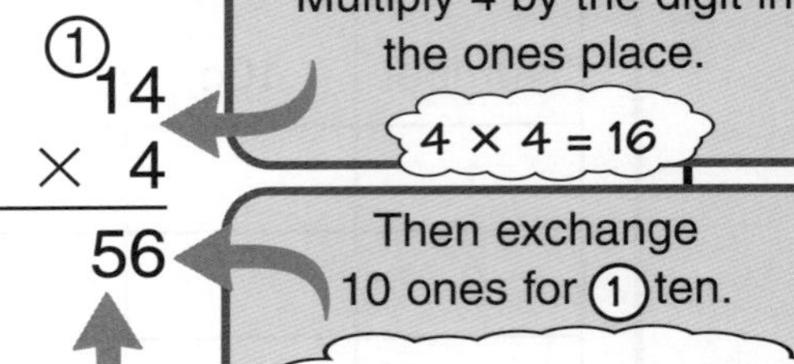

Multiply 4 by the digit in the ones place.

4 × 4 = 16

Then exchange 10 ones for ① ten.

There are 6 ones left.

Now multiply 4 by the number in the tens place and add ① ten.

Use base ten blocks to solve each problem.
Explain each step to your partner or teacher.

1. $\begin{array}{r} 13 \\ \times\ 4 \\ \hline \end{array}$ **2.** $\begin{array}{r} 15 \\ \times\ 3 \\ \hline \end{array}$ **3.** $\begin{array}{r} 23 \\ \times\ 4 \\ \hline \end{array}$ **4.** $\begin{array}{r} 25 \\ \times\ 2 \\ \hline \end{array}$

5. Draw a picture that shows how to multiply 2 × 16.

Draw 2 groups of 16.

Tens	Ones

Draw a picture ***after*** you exchange 10 ones for 1 ten.

Tens	Ones

Record what you did:

$$\begin{array}{r} 16 \\ \times\ 2 \\ \hline \end{array}$$

6. **How are the solutions for the problems 2 × 43 and 2 × 46 alike? How are they different?**

Multiplication with Two Regroupings

Camels can walk 25 miles a day. If a camel walks 25 miles each day for five days, how many miles will it travel?

Build 25 five times.

Tens	Ones

Exchange 20 ones for 2 tens.

Tens	Ones

Exchange 10 tens for 1 hundred.

Hundreds	Tens	Ones
1	2	5

Here is another way to work the problem.

$5 \times 25 = 5 \times (20 + 5) = (5 \times 20) + (5 \times 5) = 100 + 25 = 125$

Use base ten blocks and the distributive property to solve problems 1 and 2.

1. $\begin{array}{r} 36 \\ \times\ 3 \\ \hline \end{array}$

2. $\begin{array}{r} 43 \\ \times\ 4 \\ \hline \end{array}$

$3 \times 36 = 3 \times (30 + 6)$

$= \qquad + \qquad =$

Find the products. Use any method.

3. $\begin{array}{r} 27 \\ \times\ 5 \\ \hline \end{array}$

4. $\begin{array}{r} 32 \\ \times\ 5 \\ \hline \end{array}$

5. $\begin{array}{r} 17 \\ \times\ 6 \\ \hline \end{array}$

6. $\begin{array}{r} 34 \\ \times\ 7 \\ \hline \end{array}$

7. George sends 32 emails a month. How many emails does George send in 6 months? ________

8. Sophia jogs 26 miles every week. How many miles does she jog in 4 weeks? ________

TEST PREP

Tomaso buys stamps for his mother. Each stamp costs 18¢. How much money does Tomaso spend on 4 stamps?

A 22¢ Ⓐ
B 42¢ Ⓑ
C 72¢ Ⓒ
D 432¢ Ⓓ

2-Digit Multiplication with Arrays

You can use an array to show multiplication of 2-digit numbers.

Lauren is using beads to make bracelets. She puts 14 beads on each bracelet. How many beads will she need to make 3 bracelets?

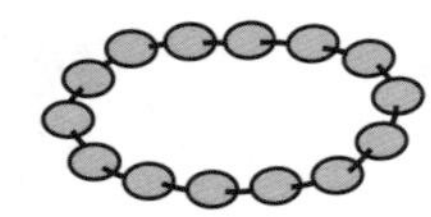
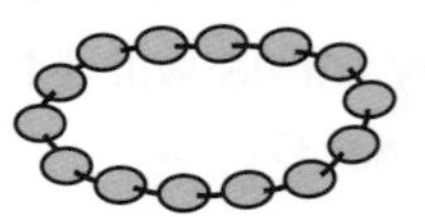
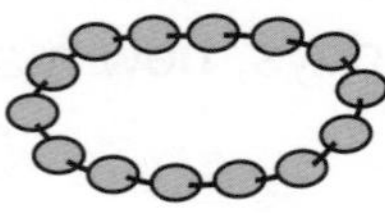

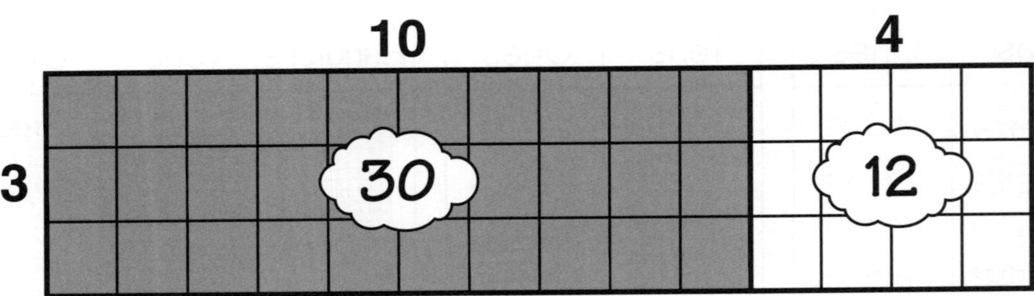

$3 \times 14 = 3 \times (10 + 4)$

$= (3 \times 10) + (3 \times 4) = 30 + 12 =$ ______

Use the arrays to solve the problems.

1.

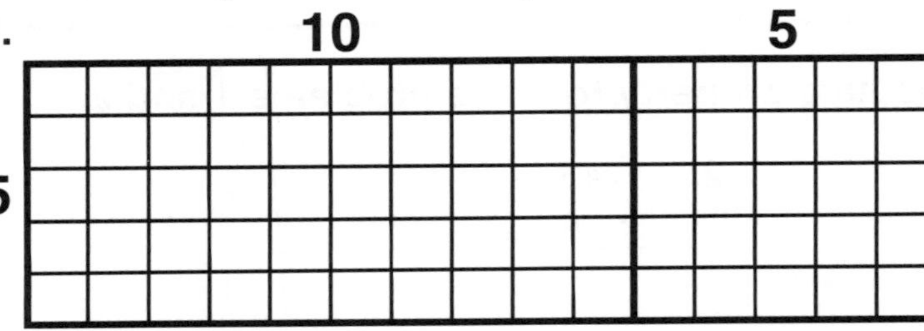

$5 \times 15 = 5 \times ($ $+$ $)$

= ______ + ______

= ______ + ______

= ______

2.

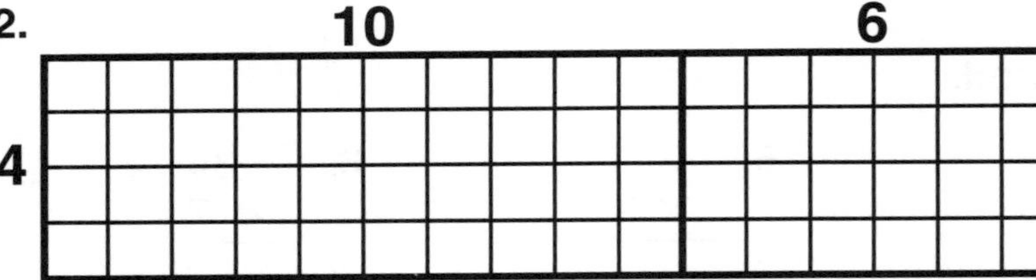

$4 \times 16 = 4 \times ($ $+$ $)$

= ______ + ______

= ______ + ______

= ______

Multiply.

3. $\begin{array}{r} 16 \\ \times\ 4 \\ \hline \end{array}$

4. $\begin{array}{r} 25 \\ \times\ 6 \\ \hline \end{array}$

5. $\begin{array}{r} 36 \\ \times\ 5 \\ \hline \end{array}$

6. $\begin{array}{r} 47 \\ \times\ 7 \\ \hline \end{array}$

7. A trucking company has big trucks called "18 wheelers." Each truck has 18 wheels. How many wheels are on 6 big trucks?

______

8. A truck travels 15 miles on 1 gallon of gas. How many miles can the truck travel on 8 gallons of gas?

______

Estimating the Product

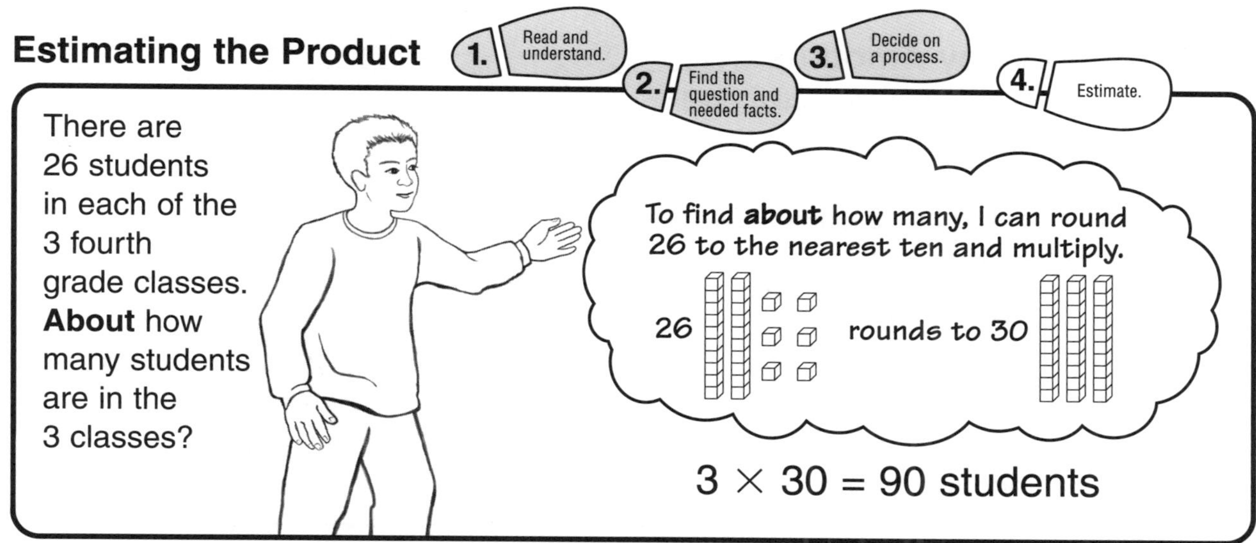

Round each number to the nearest ten.

1. 21 rounds to ______ 2. 24 rounds to ______ 3. 29 rounds to ______ 4. 25 rounds to ______

5. 32 rounds to ______ 6. 48 rounds to ______ 7. 63 rounds to ______ 8. 57 rounds to ______

Round each number to the nearest hundred.

9. 325 rounds to ______ 10. 582 rounds to ______ 11. 251 rounds to ______

12. 635 rounds to ______ 13. 411 rounds to ______ 14. 795 rounds to ______

Estimate the products by rounding the 2-digit number to the nearest ten.

	rounds to		estimate		rounds to		estimate
15. 3×49	_____	× _____	= ______	16. 4×38	_____	× _____	= ______
17. 6×21	_____	× _____	= ______	18. 5×67	_____	× _____	= ______

19. Each third grade class has 27 students. There are 4 classes of third graders. Estimate the number of third graders.

______

20. There were 74 fourth graders in the cafeteria each day on Wednesday, Thursday, and Friday. Estimate the number of fourth graders who ate in the cafeteria on all 3 days.

______

21. **The Green family eats 18 servings of fruit a week. Is it reasonable to say that this family eats more than 80 servings in 4 weeks? Explain.**

Estimating Money Amounts

1. Read and understand. 2. Find the question and needed facts. 3. Decide on a process. 4. Estimate. 5. Solve and check back.

You can round money to help make decisions.

Books cost 83¢ at the book sale. Mark has $5.00 and wants to buy 5 books. Estimate to see if he has enough money.

Book Sale 83¢ Each

83¢ is closer to 80¢ than 90¢.

5 × 80¢ = 400¢ or $4.00
Mark has enough money.

Solve.

$$\begin{array}{r} \overset{1}{83¢} \\ \times\ 5 \\ \hline \$4.15 \end{array}$$

Check your answer.
$4.15 is still less than $5.00, so he has enough money.

Estimate each product by rounding to the nearest ten.

1. 3 × 48 = _____
2. 2 × 63 = _____
3. 4 × 75 = _____
4. 6 × 74 = _____

Estimate the products by rounding to the nearest 10¢.

	rounds to		estimate
5. 7 × 68¢ =	_____	× _____	= $_______
7. 4 × 76¢ =	_____	× _____	= $ _______
6. 2 × 81¢ =	_____	× _____	= $_______
8. 9 × 42¢ =	_____	× _____	= $_______

Estimate the answer. Solve. Check for reasonableness.

9. Michelle sells magazines to raise money for her school. She earns 81¢ for each magazine she sells. She sold 9 magazines. How much did she earn?

   Est. __________ Actual __________

10. David wants to buy 8 rulers. Each ruler costs 78¢. David has $6. Does he have enough money? Yes or No?

    Est. __________ Actual __________

11. You want to buy 6 sodas for 43¢ each. You have $3. Do you have enough money? Yes or No?

    Est. __________ Actual __________

12. Mia wants to buy 7 hair ribbons for 89¢ each. She has $6. Does she have enough money? Yes or No?

    Est. __________ Actual __________

13. **In problem 11, explain if it is a good idea to round numbers down when asked the question "Do you have enough money?"**

Too Much, Too Little Information

1. Read and understand.
2. Find the question and needed facts.
3. Decide on a process.

1. Read and understand.

The Harrisons went fishing. There were 5 people in the boat. They paid $20 to rent a boat. Each person caught 7 fish. How many fish did they catch in all?

2. Find the necessary facts.

The problem has an extra fact.

3. Decide on the process.

This problem puts groups of equal size together, so it is a multiplication problem.

$$\begin{array}{r} 7 \\ \times\ 5 \\ \hline \end{array}$$

____ fish in all

Underline the question. Circle the facts. Cross out extra information. Solve. When problems do not have enough information, write the missing fact.

1. Tony drank 6 glasses of milk every day for 7 days. His sister drank 3 glasses of milk. How many glasses of milk did Tony drink?

   ____

2. Erica helped her dad chop 6 trees into logs. The job took 3 hours. They cut each tree into 9 logs. How many logs do they have altogether?

   ____

3. Mary went to summer school 4 days a week for 4 weeks. She went swimming 2 days a week. How many days did she go to summer school?

   ____

4. The radio station played Jennie's favorite song 4 times on Monday and 9 times on Tuesday. How many times did they play the song during the week?

   ____

5. Mr. Teller put 9 boxes of "Wowee" cereal on each of 9 shelves. One box of cereal costs $2.80. How many boxes of cereal were on all of the shelves?

   ____

6. The softball team has 3 practices a week. How many hours do they practice in 1 week?

   ____

7. Kurt collects baseball hats. He put 6 hats on each shelf in his bedroom. How many hats are on Kurt's shelves?

   ____

8. Miss Hall walks 2 flights of stairs to get to her office. How many steps does she take to get to her office in 5 days?

   ____

Multiplying 3-Digit Numbers by 1-Digit Numbers

A plane carries 231 passengers. The plane makes 2 full trips a day. How many passengers does the plane carry in one day?

The problem puts together groups of equal size.

Hundreds	Tens	Ones
4	6	2

I wrote it this way: first multiply 2 by the ones, then 2 by the tens, then 2 by the hundreds.

$$\begin{array}{r} 231 \\ \times \quad 2 \\ \hline 462 \end{array}$$

passengers

Draw a picture to multiply. Use a ▫ for ones, ▯ for tens, and □ for hundreds.

1. 4 × 122 = □   □ = ______

2. 3 × 232 = □   □ = ______

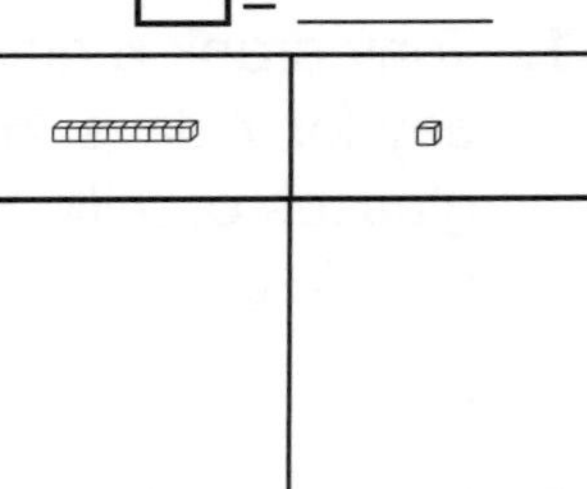

Use base ten blocks to multiply. How are the solutions to problems 4 and 5 alike? How are they different?

3. $\begin{array}{r} 122 \\ \times \quad 3 \\ \hline \end{array}$ **4.** $\begin{array}{r} 123 \\ \times \quad 2 \\ \hline \end{array}$ **5.** $\begin{array}{r} 121 \\ \times \quad 2 \\ \hline \end{array}$ **6.** $\begin{array}{r} 221 \\ \times \quad 4 \\ \hline \end{array}$

Alike: ______________________ Different: ______________________

7. There are 124 pencils in a case. How many are there in 2 cases?

____

8. Willie's grandfather saves his pennies in jars. There are 120 pennies in a full jar. How many pennies would be in 3 full jars?

____

9.  **What is the pattern for multiplying a 1-digit number by a 3-digit number?**

Multiplying 3-Digit Numbers by 1-Digit Numbers

Jake's uncle drives a delivery truck. Each week he drives a 632-mile route. How many miles does he travel in 2 weeks?

Build 2 sets of 632. Put blocks that have the same place value together. There will be 4 ones, 6 tens, and 12 hundreds.

Thousands	Hundreds	Tens	Ones

```
  632
×   2
    4  (2 × 2)
   60  (2 × 30)
 1200  (2 × 600)
 1264
```

Trade 10 hundreds for 1 thousand. There will be 4 ones, 6 tens, 2 hundreds, and 1 thousand...1264.

Thousands	Hundreds	Tens	Ones

Record:

```
  632
×   2
```

_______ miles

Multiply.

1.	2.	3.	4.	5.
312 × 4	523 × 4	316 × 5	313 × 6	343 × 4

Estimate by rounding to the nearest hundred. Solve and check for reasonableness.

6. Sam has 530 points. She needs 3 times as many points to trade for a bicycle. How many points does Sam need altogether to get the bicycle?

   Est. ________ Actual ________

7. Rick and Sue collect 312 cans a week. They collected cans for 4 weeks. How many total cans did they collect?

   Est. ________ Actual ________

Using Base Ten Blocks to Multiply

Example: 2 × 162 = 2 × (100 + 60 + 2)

Step 1: Build 2 groups of 162

Hundreds	Tens	Ones

Step 2: Exchange if possible

Hundreds	Tens	Ones

Step 3: Record

$$\begin{array}{r} \boxed{1} \\ 162 \\ \times\ \ 2 \\ \hline 324 \end{array}$$

Use base ten blocks to multiply. Draw a picture. (Use ▫ for ones, ▯ for tens, and □ for hundreds.) Then solve with paper and pencil. Compare answers.

1. 4 × 132

Step 1: Before trade

Hundreds	Tens	Ones

Step 2: After trade

Hundreds	Tens	Ones

Step 3: Record

Estimate an answer by rounding to the nearest hundred. Solve and check back.

2. There are 365 days in 1 year. How many days old would you be on your ninth birthday?

Est. ________ Actual ________

3. There are a total of 245 students in fourth and fifth grade. If all students ate lunch in the lunchroom, how many lunches will they eat in 5 days?

Est. ________ Actual ________

Write a set of directions that tell how to multiply a 3-digit number by a 1-digit number. Use the example 3 × 152 and solve it with your directions.

Multiplying Across Zero

Curt lives 306 miles from his grandmother. How many miles does he travel on a round trip?

Build 2 sets of 306. There will be 12 ones, 0 tens, and 6 hundreds.

$$\begin{array}{r} 306 \\ \times \quad 2 \\ \hline \end{array}$$

HUNDREDS	TENS	ONES

Exchange 10 ones for 1 ten. There will be 2 ones, 1 ten, and 6 hundreds ... 612.

HUNDREDS	TENS	ONES

Record:

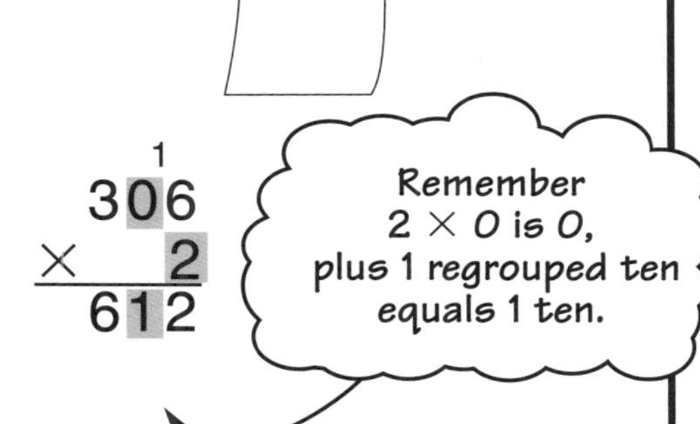

$$\begin{array}{r} {}^{1} \\ 306 \\ \times \quad 2 \\ \hline 612 \end{array}$$

Remember 2 × 0 is 0, plus 1 regrouped ten equals 1 ten.

_______ miles

Find the products.

1. $\begin{array}{r} 101 \\ \times \ 5 \\ \hline \end{array}$
2. $\begin{array}{r} 203 \\ \times \ 3 \\ \hline \end{array}$
3. $\begin{array}{r} 304 \\ \times \ 2 \\ \hline \end{array}$
4. $\begin{array}{r} 402 \\ \times \ 3 \\ \hline \end{array}$
5. $\begin{array}{r} 805 \\ \times \ 7 \\ \hline \end{array}$
6. $\begin{array}{r} 704 \\ \times \ 6 \\ \hline \end{array}$
7. $\begin{array}{r} 604 \\ \times \ 9 \\ \hline \end{array}$
8. $\begin{array}{r} 705 \\ \times \ 8 \\ \hline \end{array}$

9. The fourth graders had a fundraiser for the homeless. They raised $105 every month for 9 months. How much did they raise in all?

   Est. ________ Actual ________

10. The fifth graders collected $204 for the Special Olympics each month. How much money did they collect in 9 months?

    Est. ________ Actual ________

Your friend multiplied 4 × 306. He said the product is 1264. Use numbers and words to explain to your friend if his answer is right or wrong. If it is wrong, explain the error that your friend made.

Multiplying by 10 and Multiples of 10

There are 25 members in the band. Mrs. Gomez wants to buy a cookie to give to each member after the concert.

Each cookie costs 10¢. How much will the cookies cost?

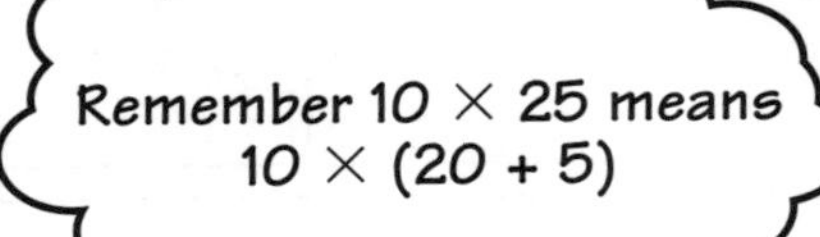

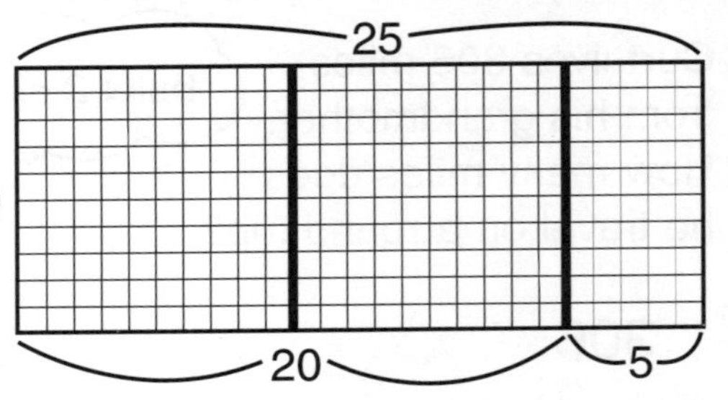

10¢ × 25 = (10¢ × 20) + (10¢ × 5)

= ________ + ________

= ________¢ or

$ ________

Look for the pattern for multiplying 10 or a multiple of 10 by any number as you solve these problems.

1. 10 × 10 = ________

2. 15 × 10 = ________

3. 37 × 10 = ________

4. 40 × 20¢ = ________

5. 20 × 30¢ = ________

6. 50 × 10¢ = ________

7. 50×30

8. 10×40

9. 60×20

10. 30×20

11. 40 × 30 = ________

12. 30 × 20 = ________

13. Most children breathe 30 times a minute. How many times will they breathe in 10 minutes?

____

14. The average person blinks 25 times a minute. How many times will the average person blink in 10 minutes?

____

15. An average heart beats about 70 times a minute. How many times will it beat in 10 minutes?

____

16. Eggs cost 10¢ each. Find the cost of 2 dozen eggs.

____

17.  **What is the pattern for multiplying multiples of 10 by each other? Use the example 20 × 30 to explain.**

Problem Solving: Draw a Picture

Every multiplication fact can be modeled as an array. The sides of the array are the factors. The total number of square units is the product.

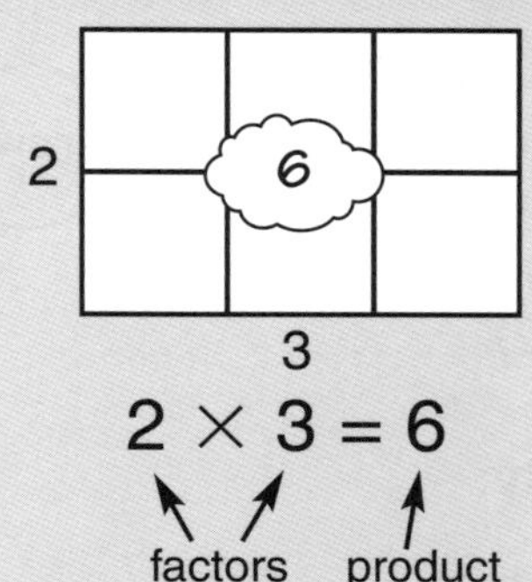

$2 \times 3 = 6$

factors product

Multiplication of larger numbers can be modeled in the same way.

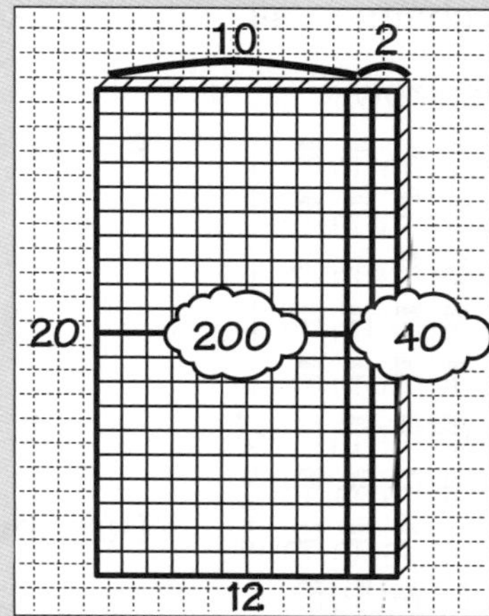

$$\begin{array}{r} 12 \\ \times\ 20 \\ \hline \end{array} = \begin{array}{r} 10 + 2 \\ \times\ 20 \\ \hline \end{array}$$

$$\begin{array}{rr} 20 \times 2 = & 40 \\ 20 \times 10 = & 200 \\ \hline & 240 \end{array}$$

Use base ten blocks on centimeter graph paper to find each product.

1. $30 \times 20 =$ ______
2. $40 \times 50 =$ ______
3. $70 \times 30 =$ ______

Find the products.

4. $20 \times 14 =$ ______
5. $30 \times 12 =$ ______
6. $40 \times 21 =$ ______

7. $\begin{array}{r} 34 \\ \times\ 20 \\ \hline \end{array}$

8. $\begin{array}{r} 23 \\ \times\ 30 \\ \hline \end{array}$

9. $\begin{array}{r} 43 \\ \times\ 20 \\ \hline \end{array}$

10. $\begin{array}{r} 11 \\ \times\ 50 \\ \hline \end{array}$

11. A frozen juice bar costs 20¢. How much would 2 dozen frozen juice bars cost? ______

12. A hippopotamus can eat 90 pounds of grass a day. How many pounds of grass will a hippopotamus eat in 20 days? ______

TEST PREP

$\begin{array}{r} 70 \\ \times\ 40 \\ \hline \end{array}$

A 280
B 470
C 1100
D 2800

Ⓐ Ⓑ Ⓒ Ⓓ

Multiplying a 2-Digit Number by a 2-Digit Number

The band members set up 13 rows of chairs with 12 chairs in each row for the concert. How many chairs in all?

I know how to multiply 3 x 12 and I know how to multiply 10 x 12.

12 chairs in each row

10 × 12

3 × 12

13 rows

Partial Productss:

13 is 10 rows of 12 and 3 rows of 12.

$$\begin{array}{rl} 12 & \\ \times\ 13 & \\ \hline 36 & (3 \times 12) \\ +\ 120 & (10 \times 12) \\ \hline \end{array}$$

Distributive Property:

$13 \times 12 = 13 \times (10 + 2)$

$= (13 \times 10) + (13 \times 2)$

= ______ chairs

Use the partial products method to find the number of chairs.

1. There are 12 chairs in each row, and 11 rows.

   10 rows of 12 =
   + 1 row of 12 =

   $$\begin{array}{r} 12 \\ \times\ 11 \\ \hline \end{array}$$

   ____

2. There are 12 chairs in each row, and 14 rows.

   10 rows of 12 =
   + 4 rows of 12 =

   ____

3. The band members sold small plants to raise money to repair their instruments. Each crate of plants had 16 rows with 12 plants in each row. How many plants are in one crate?

   Est. ________ Actual ________

4. Nick practices the trumpet 15 minutes each day. How many minutes does he practice in 2 weeks?

   Est. ________ Actual ________

Draw an array on graph paper to show the multiplication problem 12 × 14. Use the array to find the product. Explain in numbers and words.

Multiplying 2-Digit Numbers

This problem puts groups of the same size together. We multiply 12 X 62.

An orange grove has 62 rows of orange trees. There are 12 trees in each row. How many orange trees are there in all?

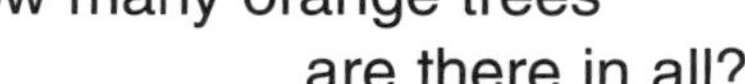

$$\begin{array}{r} 62 \\ \times\ 12 \\ \hline 124 \\ +\ 620 \\ \hline \end{array}$$

(12 = 10 + 2)

124 ← Multiply 2 by 62.

+ 620 ← Multiply 10 by 62.

← Add to find number of trees.

Find the products.

1. $\begin{array}{r} 40 \\ \times\ 29 \\ \hline \end{array}$

2. $\begin{array}{r} 58 \\ \times\ 37 \\ \hline \end{array}$

3. $\begin{array}{r} 43 \\ \times\ 35 \\ \hline \end{array}$

4. $\begin{array}{r} 48 \\ \times\ 14 \\ \hline \end{array}$

5. Mary filled 16 bags with candy. She put 14 pieces of candy in each bag. How many pieces of candy did she use?

Est. ________ Actual ________

6. A movie-plex has 12 theaters. Each theater has 75 seats. How many seats does the movie-plex have?

Est. ________ Actual ________

7. A grocery store ordered 25 crates of oranges. Each crate has 30 oranges. How many oranges did the store order?

Est. ________ Actual ________

8. The Johnstons bought 15 rolls of film for a road trip. Each roll of film holds 24 pictures. How many pictures can the Johnstons take on their trip?

Est. ________ Actual ________

TEST PREP

$\begin{array}{r} 57 \\ \times\ 34 \\ \hline \end{array}$

A 399 Ⓐ
B 1718 Ⓑ
C 1738 Ⓒ
D 1938 Ⓓ

Reasonable Estimates

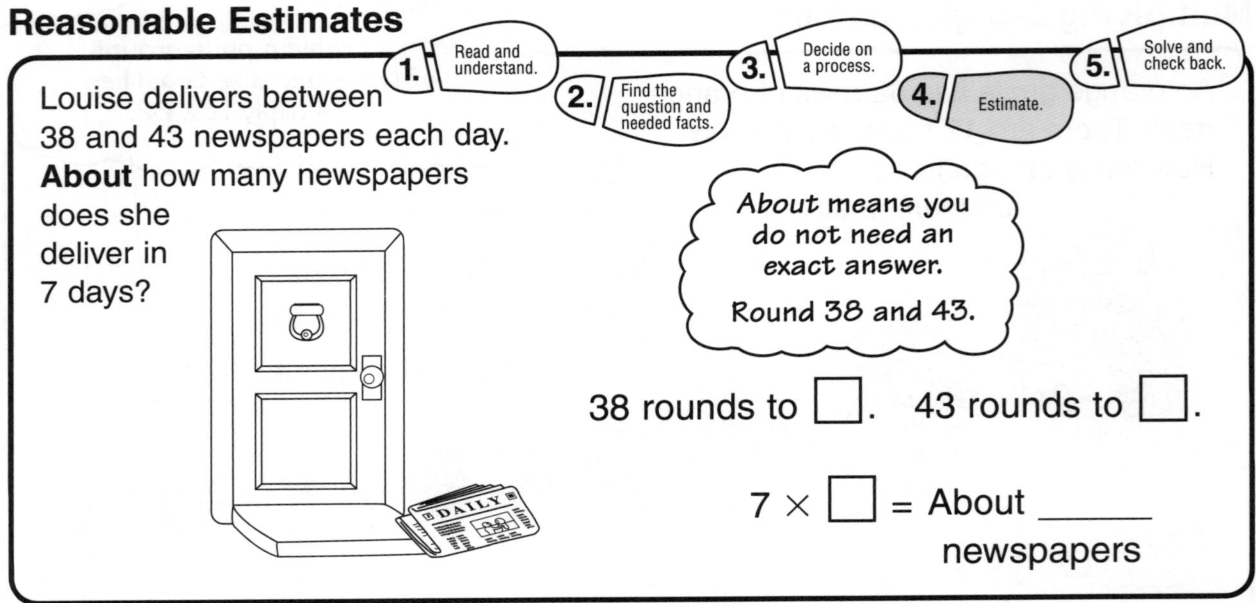

Louise delivers between 38 and 43 newspapers each day. **About** how many newspapers does she deliver in 7 days?

38 rounds to ☐. 43 rounds to ☐.

7 × ☐ = About ______ newspapers

Estimate the product. Find the actual answer.

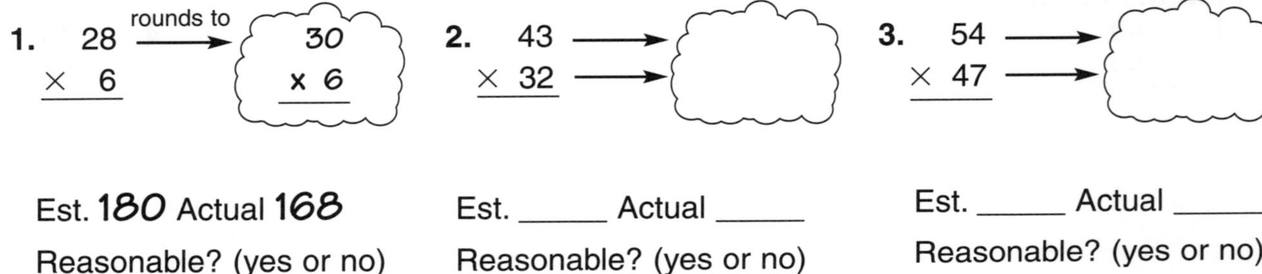

Est. 180 Actual 168
Reasonable? (yes or no)

Est. ______ Actual ______
Reasonable? (yes or no)

Est. ______ Actual ______
Reasonable? (yes or no)

4. The Art Club uses 12 tubes of paint each day. How many tubes of paint do they use in 24 days?

   Est. ______ Actual ______
   Reasonable? __________

5. The 38 members of the Art Club sell candy bars as a fundraiser. Each member sold 29 candy bars. How many candy bars did the club sell?

   Est. ______ Actual ______
   Reasonable? __________

The hardware store sold 10 screwdrivers for different prices. The least expensive one cost $9. The most expensive one cost $12. Which is the most reasonable estimate for how much money the hardware store received for selling 10 screwdrivers?

A $21 **B** $90 **C** $100 **D** $120

Explain why the other three choices are ***not*** reasonable.

Multiplying Money

Money amounts can be recorded in 2 ways: with a ¢ sign or with a $ sign and a decimal point.

Willie bought 2 small notebooks for 29¢ each. He gave the clerk a $1 bill. How much change should he receive?

58¢

Step 1:

$$\begin{array}{r} 29¢ \\ \times\ 2 \\ \hline 58¢ \end{array}$$

Step 2:

$$\begin{array}{r} 100¢ \\ -\ 58¢ \\ \hline \end{array}$$

Step 1:

$$\begin{array}{r} \$0.29 \\ \times\ 2 \\ \hline \$0.58 \end{array}$$

Step 2:

$$\begin{array}{r} \$1.00 \\ -\ \$0.58 \\ \hline \end{array}$$

Find the products. Write your answer in two ways: with a ¢ sign and a $ sign.

1. 35¢ × 2 = 70¢ ; $0.70
2. 64¢ × 5 = ______ ; ______
3. $1.25 × 3 = ______ ; ______
4. $2.40 × 6 = ______ ; ______

5. Ong bought 5 pencils that were 12¢ each. How much did the pencils cost in all?

   ______ ______

6. Nick bought 4 large notebooks that were 85¢ each. How much did the notebooks cost in all?

   ______ ______

7. In *Tales of a Fourth Grade Nothing,* Mom takes Peter and Fudge to a movie. If Mom and Peter each get popcorn for 29¢, how much change did they get back from a $1 bill?

   ______ ______

8. Peter got a dog and named him Turtle. If Peter bought 2 bags of dog treats for $1.85 each, how much change would he get back from a $5 bill?

   ______ ______

You finish the story. Ask a mathematical question. Then find the answer.

9. Nick and Willie went shopping in the music store. They had $10.00. They found sheet music on sale for $3.25.

   ____

   ______

10. Ong had $20.00. She wanted to buy CDs for $6.50 each.

   ____

   ______

Two-Step Problems Using Parentheses

Parentheses ( ) are symbols used in number sentences to show which operation should be done first.

Barbara bought 3 small notebooks at 29¢ each. She gave the clerk a \$5.00 bill. How much change did she receive?

79¢ 32¢ glue 29¢ 20¢

Step 1
Multiply 3 × 29¢

Step 2
Subtract the answer in Step 1 from \$5.00

You can write a number sentence with parentheses to solve the problem.

$$\begin{array}{r} 29¢ \\ \times\ 3 \\ \hline \_\_\_\ ¢ \end{array} \qquad \begin{array}{r} \$5.00 \\ -\ \_\_\_\_ \\ \hline \$\ \_\_\_\_ \end{array}$$

☐ = \$5.00 – (3 × 29¢)

☐ = \$5.00 – _______

☐ = _______

Use the pictures and prices of the items above to write two-step number sentences to solve each problem. Use parentheses to show what to do first.

1. You buy 1 ruler and 1 notebook and pay with a \$1.00 bill. How much do you have left?

No. sentence: ☐ = ________________

☐ = ____________

☐ = ________

2. You buy 2 jars of glue and pay with a \$1.00 bill. How much do you have left?

No. sentence: ☐ = ________________

☐ = ____________

☐ = ________

3. You buy 1 jar of glue and 1 box of crayons and pay with a \$5.00 bill. How much do you have left?

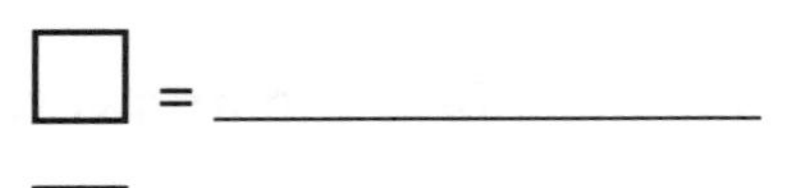

No. sentence: ☐ = ________________

☐ = ____________

☐ = ________

4. You buy 2 rulers and a notebook. You pay with a \$5.00 bill. How much do you have left?

No. sentence: ☐ = ________________

☐ = ____________

☐ = ________

5.  **How do parentheses help when you are solving two-step problems?**

$n=?$

Finding Factors

The numbers being multiplied in a multiplication problem are called the **factors**. You can make arrays to find the factors of a number.

You are packing 12 square pieces of candy in one-layer, rectangular boxes. You might pack them in a long, thin box that has one row of 12 candies.

What other ways might you pack the candies? Draw pictures of the different ways.

List the possible sides of a box with 12 candies: 1, 12, ___, ___, ___, ___.

List the multiplication facts that equal 12: 1 × 12, ______, ______.

The numbers on the sides of the box of 12 candies are the same as the numbers that make the multiplication facts that equal 12.

These numbers are called the "factors" of 12.

List the factors of 12: 1, 12, ______, ______, ______, ______.

Use square tiles to find the factors of each number. Draw a rectangular picture and write the factors for each number.

1. 8 : 1 × 8 2 × 4

Factors: 1, 8, 2, 4

2. 6 :

Factors: ____________

3. 3 :

Factors: ____________

4. 9 :

Factors: ____________

5. 10 :

Factors: ____________

6. 16 :

Factors: ____________

7. 20 :

Factors: ____________

8. 24 :

Factors: ____________

Prime Numbers: Only One Rectangular Shape

A **prime number** has only one array.

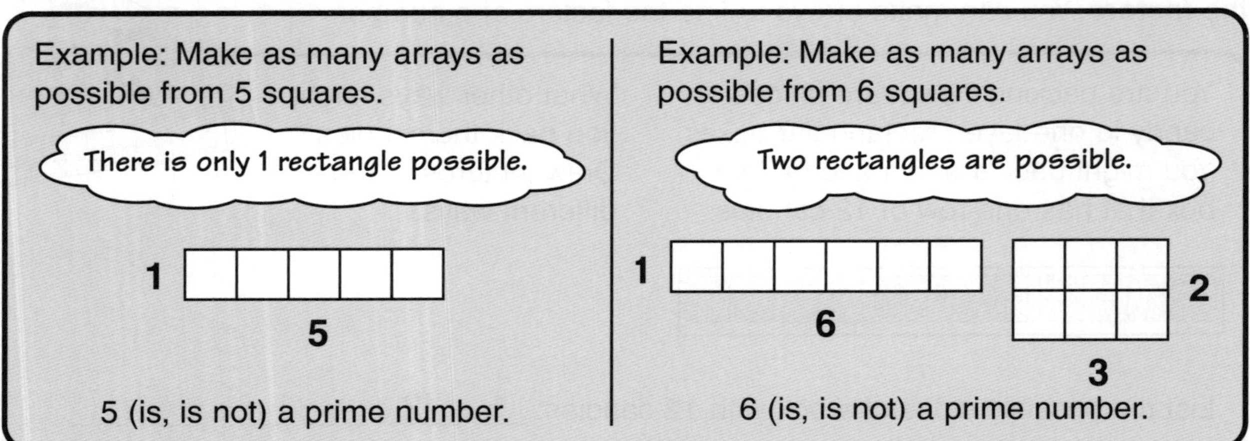

Use cubes or cut out squares to find if each number is prime or not prime. Circle the correct answer.

1. Use 2 squares or cubes.

Arrays: 1 × 2 (or 2 × 1)

prime   not prime

2. Use 3 squares or cubes.

Arrays: ___________

prime   not prime

3. Use 4 squares or cubes.

Arrays: ___________

prime   not prime

4. Use 7 squares or cubes.

Arrays: ___________

prime   not prime

5. Shade the numbers that are prime.

1	2	3	4	5	6	7	8	9	10
11	12	13	14	15	16	17	18	19	20
21	22	23	24	25	26	27	28	29	30

TEST PREP

What number is <u>not</u> prime?

A 3 Ⓐ
B 4 Ⓑ
C 5 Ⓒ
D 7 Ⓓ

Using Letters as Variables in an Expression

An expression is a part of a number sentence. You can write an expression with an operational sign such as +, –, ×, or ÷, and a variable such as a □ or the letter n.

A **variable** is a symbol that can stand for an unknown number. A variable may be used with a plus or minus sign to show addition or subtraction.

Santo saves his pennies in a can that he keeps on his dresser. How many pennies are in the can?

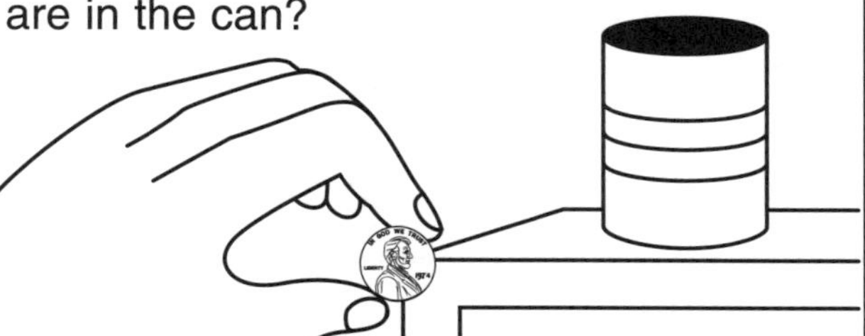

The number of pennies is not known. The letter n can be used to stand for the unknown number. The letter n is called a variable.

= ?

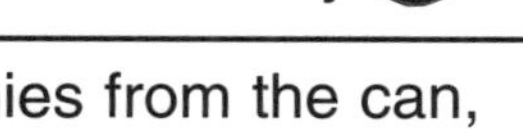

If Santo puts 4 pennies into the can, how many pennies would be in the can?

There would be $n + 4$ pennies.

If Santo takes 5 pennies from the can, how many pennies would be in the can?

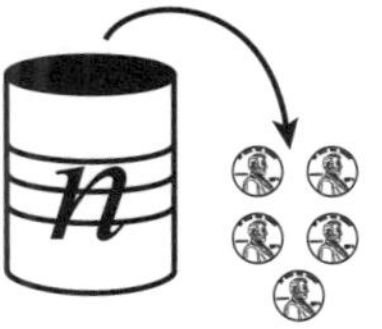

There would be $n - 5$ pennies.

Write an algebraic expression for each picture. Use n for the variable.

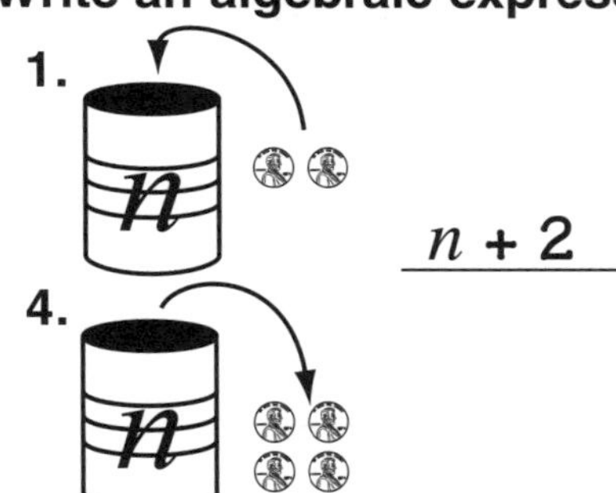

1. $n + 2$

2. 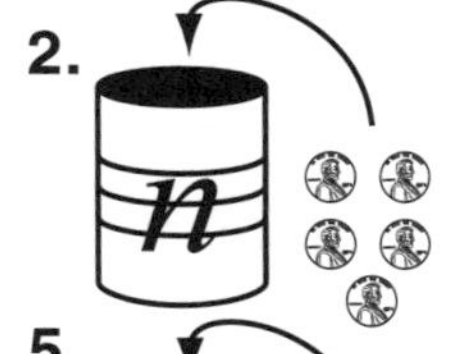 ________

3. 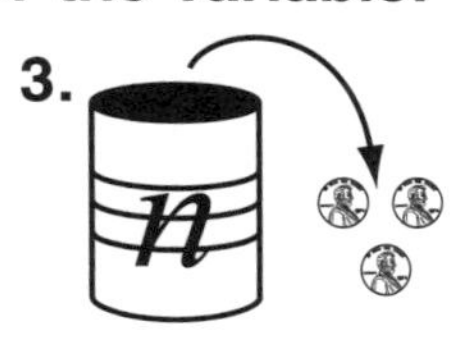 $n - 3$

4. ________

5. 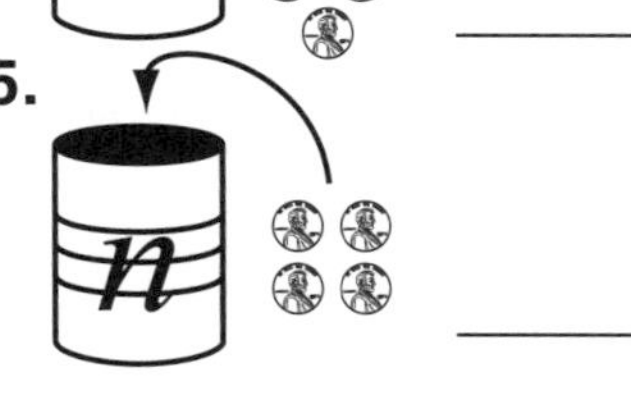 ________

6. 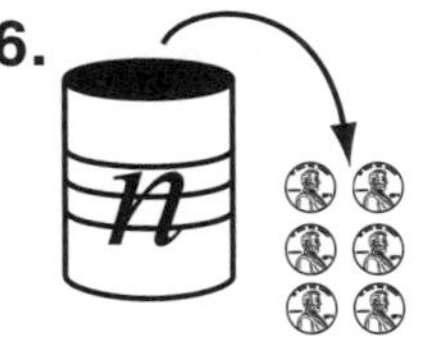 ________

Write an expression with n for each phrase.

7. a number plus 4 ________
8. a number less 6 ________
9. a number decreased by 2 ________
10. a number increased by 7 ________
11. 20 plus a number n ________
12. a number minus 10 ________
13. 5 more than a number ________
14. 4 less than a number ________
15. 6 increased by a number ________
16. the sum of 9 and a number ________
17. a number minus 8 ________
18. difference between a number and 5 ________
19. 10 minus a number ________
20. the sum of 6 and a number ________

n=?

Using Letters as Variables in a Number Sentence or Equation

A number sentence or equation includes an expression and an equals sign.
A number sentence has an equals sign and an expression does not.

Write an expression for the words:	Write a number sentence or equation for the words:
The product of 4 and a number n.	The product of 4 and n is 8.
$4 \times n$	4 × what number is 8? $4 \times n = 8$ $4 \times 2 = 8$ so $n = 2$

Write an expression for the words.

1. The sum of 8 and 4.

   ____

2. The difference of 10 and n.

   ____

3. The product of 3 and a number.

   ____

4. The sum of a number and 5.

   ____

Write a number sentence using the letter *n*. Solve for *n*.

5. Three times a number is 30.

   ____

   $n =$ ______

6. The sum of a number and 10 is 15.

   ____

   $n =$ ______

7. The product of 4 and a number is 28.

   ____

   $n =$ ______

8. A number plus 8 is 15.

   ____

   $n =$ ______

Find the missing factor.

9. $n \times 4 = 12$ $n =$ ______

10. $2 \times n = 12$ $n =$ ______

11. $4 \times n = 0$ $n =$ ______

12. $n \times 2 = 18$ $n =$ ______

Solve.

13. $2 \times \square = 3 + 5$

14. $4 + 8 = 3 \times \square$

Meaning of Division

Division means to share or break a number apart into groups of equal size.

Fred and his friends collect sports cards from cereal boxes. They have collected 12 sports cards. If Fred and a friend share the cards equally, how many cards will each person receive?

There are 12 cards shared by 2 people, so each person gets ____ cards. 12 ÷ 2 = ☐

3 friends: 12 ÷ 3 = _______ cards

4 friends: 12 ÷ 4 = _______ cards

6 friends: 12 ÷ 6 = _______ cards

12 friends: 12 ÷ 12 = _______ cards

Complete the tables to show the different ways to share the cards.

1. Share 10 sports cards.

Total Cards	Number of Friends	Division Fact	Cards for Each Friend
10	2	10 ÷ 2 =	5
10	5		
10	10		
10	1	10 ÷ 1 =	10

2. Share 8 sports cards.

Total Cards	Number of Friends	Division Fact	Cards for Each Friend
8	2		
8	4		
8	8		
8	1		

Write a division sentence to solve each problem.

3. There are 10 children on the playground. The group is divided equally into 2 teams. How many children are on each team?

____

4. The teacher put 20 students into 4 reading groups of equal size. How many students were in each group?

____

5. The Girl Scout leader put the 20 scouts into 5 groups of equal size. How many Girl Scouts were in each small group?

____

6. The after school chess club has 12 members. Each chessboard is for 2 players. How many boards are needed?

____

7. **What does division mean?**

Division as Separating Groups of Equal Size

Division may be used to find how many groups of equal size may be formed from a large number.

Twenty friends go to the park. They form teams of 5 to play basketball. How many teams can be formed?

😊😑😐🙂😌😊😑😐🙂😌
😑🙂😐🙂😊😑🙂😐🙂😊

Circle groups of 5.

There are 20 players divided into

teams of 5: ______ groups

$20 \div 5 =$ _____ teams

quotient

The answer in division is the **quotient.**

Separate each group into teams of the given number.

Number in Group	Number of Teams	Division Fact	Quotient
10	2	$10 \div 2 =$	
14	2		
15	5		

Number in Group	Number of Teams	Division Fact	Quotient
20	5		
12	4		
12	3		

Circle groups of equal size.

7. How many groups of 2 are in 8?

O O O O
O O O O

____

8. How many groups of 5 are in 10?

O O O O O
O O O O O

____

9. The skating club forms pairs of students for a contest. How many pairs can be formed with 18 students?

____

10. A hockey team is made of 5 players. How many teams can be formed with 30 players?

____

TEST PREP

Choose the correct number sentence for the picture.

(XXXXX)
(XXXXX)
(XXXXX)
(XXXXX)

A $20 + 5 = 25$ Ⓐ
B $20 - 5 = 15$ Ⓑ
C $20 \times 5 = 100$ Ⓒ
D $20 \div 5 = 4$ Ⓓ

Dividing by 2 and 5

Division may be written two ways: as a number sentence using ÷ or as a division "house" $\overline{)\quad}$.

Fred's class is making lemon cakes for a bake sale. They need 2 eggs to make each cake. How many cakes can they make with 8 eggs?

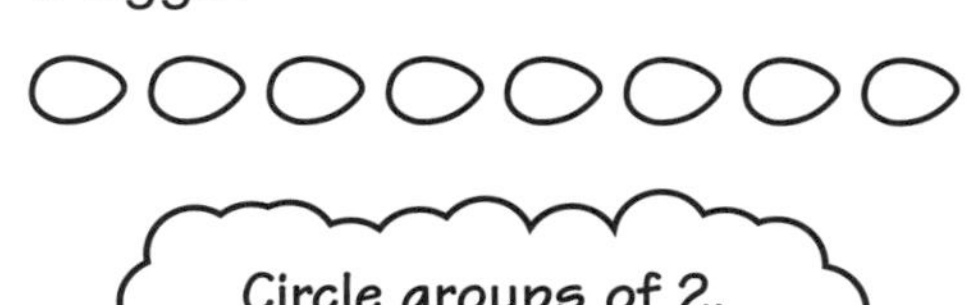

$8 \div 2$ or $2\overline{)8}$

The students earned $30 from the bake sale. The money will be divided equally among 5 rooms. How many dollars will each room get?

$30 ÷ 5 = $_____ or $5\overline{)30}$

Circle groups of the same size. Write the division solution in two different ways.

1. Groups of 5.

___ ÷ ___ = ___ $\overline{)\quad}$

2. Groups of 2.

___ ÷ ___ = ___ $\overline{)\quad}$

Solve.

3. 6 ÷ 2 = _____

4. 12 ÷ 2 = _____

5. 10 ÷ 5 = _____

6. $2\overline{)14}$

7. $5\overline{)20}$

8. $5\overline{)25}$

Use the table of multiples to find a pattern for numbers that can be divided **evenly** by 2 and 5.

×	0	1	2	3	4	5	6	7	8	9
2	0	2	4	6	8	10	12	14	16	18
5	0	5	10	15	20	25	30	35	40	45

9. Numbers that divide evenly by 2 will end in ______, ______, ______, ______, ______.

10. Numbers that divide evenly by 5 will end in ______ or ______.

Division and Multiplication as Opposites

Multiplication puts groups of equal size together.

2 groups of 5 is 10.

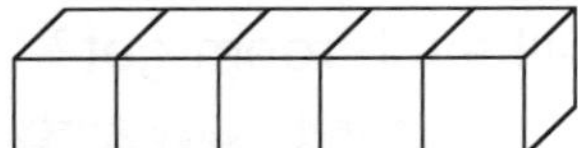 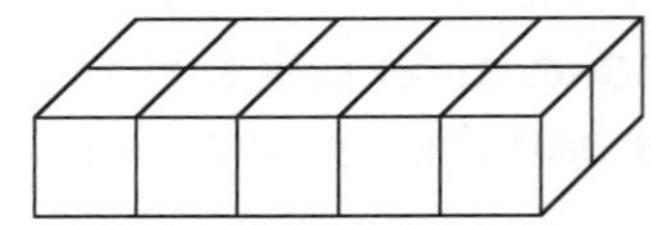

$$\begin{array}{r} 5 \\ \times 2 \\ \hline 10 \end{array}$$

Division takes groups of equal size away from a number.

10 divided into 2 groups is 5.

$$2\overline{)10}$$ = 5

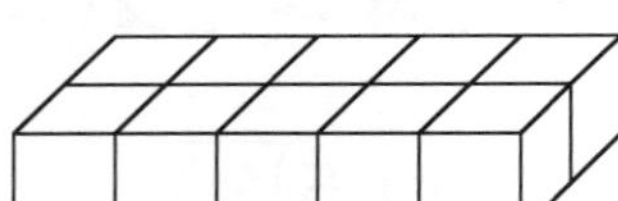 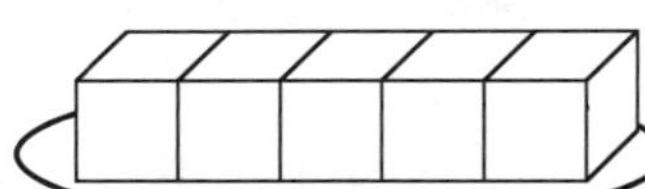 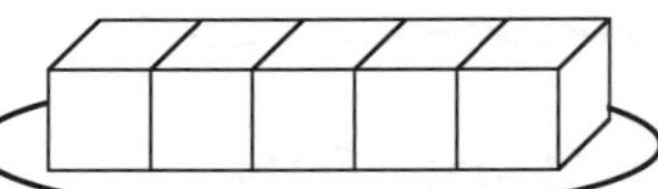

Write a division fact for each multiplication fact.

1. $2 \times 4 = 8$ $2\overline{)8}$ = 4
2. $5 \times 3 = 15$
3. $4 \times 3 = 12$
4. $2 \times 9 = 18$
5. $3 \times 6 = 18$
6. $8 \times 2 = 16$
7. $4 \times 7 = 28$
8. $9 \times 3 = 27$
9. $18 \div 2 =$ ______

10. $30 \div 5 =$ ______

Think: 5 × ______ = 30

11. $45 \div 5 =$ ______

12. 12 cookies 6 

How many 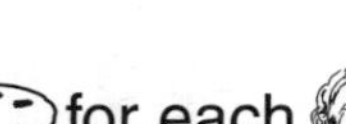 for each girl?

____

13. 8 ears 2 on each 

How many  ?

____

Explain what we mean when we say, "Multiplication and division are opposites." Use words, pictures, and symbols to explain with this example.

$6 \times 2 = 12$ and $12 \div 2 = 6$

The Role of 1 and 0 in Division

You can find patterns when you divide by 1 and 0. You can also find patterns when you divide a number by itself.

3 children divided into 1 car.

 = ☐ number of people in each car.

3 ÷ 1 = ☐

A number divided by 1 equals ____________.

3 children divided into 3 cars.

 = ☐ number of people in each car.

3 ÷ 3 = ☐

A number divided by itself equals ____.

0 children divided into 3 cars.

= ☐ number of people in each car.

0 ÷ 3 = ☐

Zero divided by any number equals ___.

3 children divided into 0 cars.

= no cars number of people in each car.

3 ÷ 0 = cannot do

A number divided by 0 equals cannot do.

Divide. When you divide by zero, write "cannot do" or CND as the answer.

1. 3 ÷ 3 = _______ **2.** 0 ÷ 3 = _______ **3.** 1 ÷ 1 = _______ **4.** 0 ÷ 7 = _______

5. 8 ÷ 1 = _______ **6.** 2 ÷ 2 = _______ **7.** 4 ÷ 4 = _______ **8.** 2 ÷ 0 = CND

9. $4\overline{)4}$ $1\overline{)3}$ $2\overline{)2}$ $5\overline{)5}$ $1\overline{)4}$ $1\overline{)5}$

10. $0\overline{)5}$ $4\overline{)0}$ $2\overline{)0}$ $0\overline{)2}$ $5\overline{)0}$ $0\overline{)3}$

11. 0 divided by any number (except 0) is __________.

12. Any number divided by itself is __________.

13. Any number divided by 1 is _______________.

14. Division by 0. ______________

Division: Repeated Subtraction

You can use repeated subtraction to find the number of groups of the same size. Division is a shortcut for subtracting groups of equal size.

Juan has 12 cans of juice. He is packing 4 cans into each bag. How many bags will Juan use?

12 ÷ 4 means how many groups of 4 can be taken from 12.

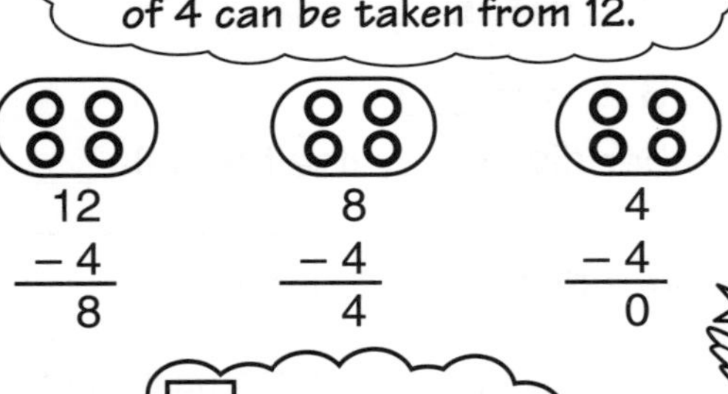

□ groups of four can be taken from 12.

It's easier to learn division facts than to do a lot of subtracting.

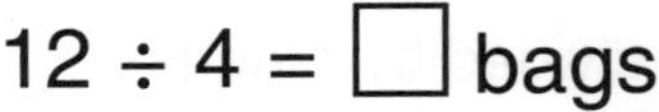

1. You have 25 pennies. You trade the pennies for nickels. How many nickels do you have? ________

2. You are trading 15 pennies for nickels. How many nickels will you have? ________

3. Subtract 2 from 12 until 0 remains.

   $12 - 2 \quad 10 - 2 \quad 8 - 2 \quad 6 - 2 \quad 4 - 2 \quad 2 - 2$

   How many groups of 2 can be subtracted from 12? ________

4. Subtract 4 from 20 until 0 remains.

   $20 - 4 \quad 16 - 4 \quad - 4 \quad - 4 \quad - 4$

   How many groups of 4 can be subtracted from 20? ________

5. $2\overline{)6}$	**6.** $3\overline{)12}$	**7.** $4\overline{)12}$	**8.** $5\overline{)35}$
9. $4\overline{)4}$	**10.** $3\overline{)18}$	**11.** $1\overline{)5}$	**12.** $3\overline{)0}$

13. Nate sells hats for $5. Nate's uncle has $20 to buy hats. How many hats can he buy? ________

14. A box of cereal costs $4. How many boxes can you buy for $20? ________

Use words, pictures, and numbers to find 15 ÷ 3 by using subtraction.

Relating Division to a Number Line

Paul Bunyan has a tree that is 12 feet long. He wants to cut 4-foot logs from the tree. How many logs can he cut?

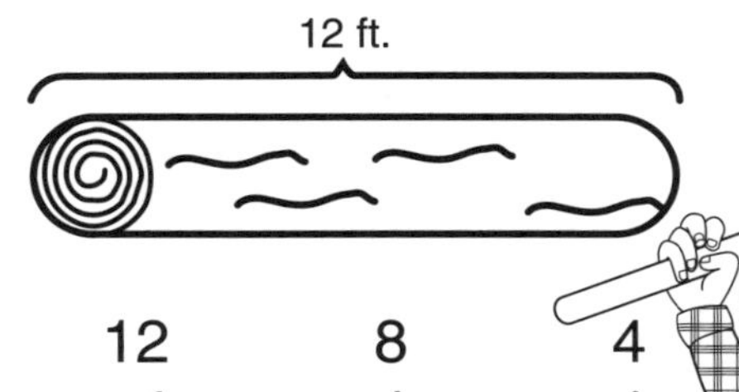

12 − 4 = 8 8 − 4 = 4 4 − 4 = 0

Paul can cut _______ logs.

I can use a number line to show the subtraction. How many jumps of 4 from 12 to 0?

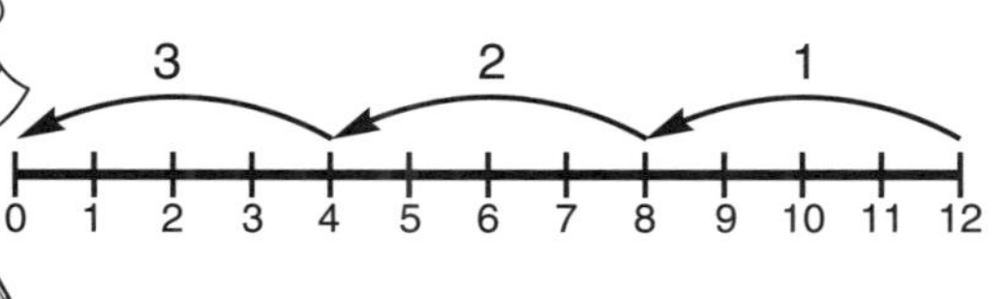

$12 \div 4 = \square$ $4\overline{)12}$

Use a number line to solve.

1. How many 4-foot logs can be cut from a 20-foot tree? ________

2. How many 3-foot logs can be cut from a 15-foot tree? ________

3. 16 ÷ 4 = ________
4. 28 ÷ 4 = ________
5. 36 ÷ 4 = ________
6. 12 ÷ 3 = ________
7. 24 ÷ 3 = ________
8. 18 ÷ 3 = ________
9. $4\overline{)24}$
10. $4\overline{)8}$
11. $4\overline{)32}$
12. $4\overline{)20}$
13. $3\overline{)15}$
14. $3\overline{)9}$
15. $3\overline{)27}$
16. $3\overline{)21}$
17. The fourth grade class is renting row boats. Each row boat holds 4 people. How many row boats must they rent for 32 people? ________
18. The fifth grade class is renting canoes at the class picnic. If each canoe holds 3 students, how many canoes must they rent for 21 students? ________

Fact Families in a Multiplication Table

A fact family is a set of related multiplication and division facts. You can use a multiplication table to find fact families.

Tennis balls are packaged in cans. Each can holds 3 tennis balls. How many cans are needed to hold 12 tennis balls?

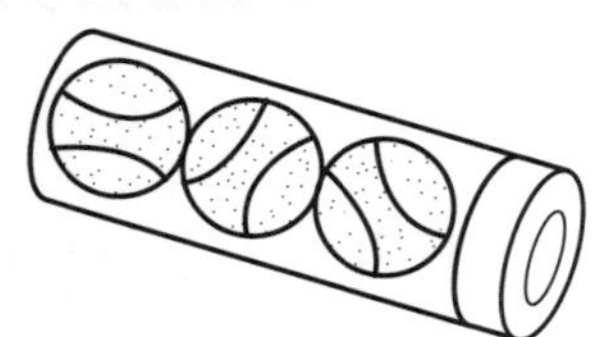

You can also use a multiplication table to divide.

Find 12 in the 3 row.
Look up to find 4.

×	0	1	2	3	4	5
0	0	0	0	0	0	0
1	0	1	2	3	4	5
2	0	2	4	6	8	10
3	0	3	6	9	(12)	15
4	0	4	8	12	16	20
5	0	5	10	15	20	25

$3\overline{)12}$ or $12 \div 3 =$ ____ cans

The multiplication table shows a family of 3 related numbers: 3, 4, and 12. These numbers make 4 facts.

2 multiplication facts

$3 \times 4 = 12$ $4 \times 3 = 12$

2 division facts

$12 \div 3 = 4$ $12 \div 4 = 3$

Use the multiplication table above to write a family of 4 facts for the 3 given numbers.

1. 2, 4, 8 $2 \times 4 = 8$ ______ ______ ______

2. 3, 5, 15 ______ ______ ______ ______

3. 3, 2, 6 ______ ______ ______ ______

4. 4, 5, 20 ______ ______ ______ ______

Write the missing number for each triangle fact card.

5.

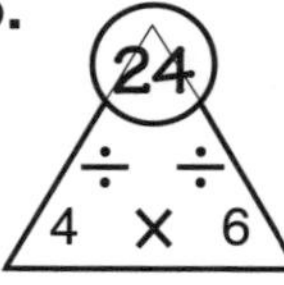

15
÷ ÷
× 3

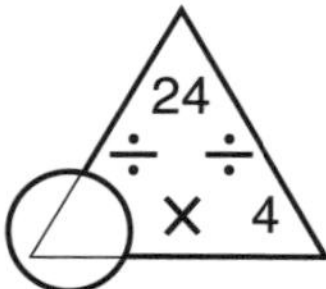

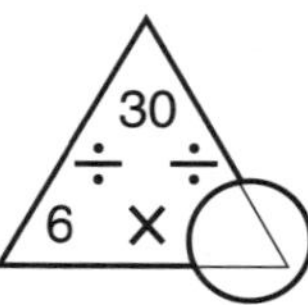

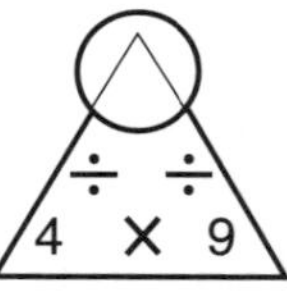

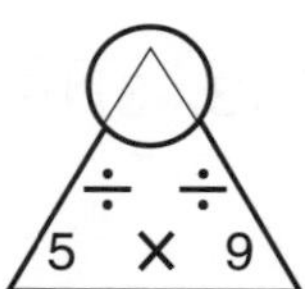

TEST PREP

The figure below is a model for $3 \times 6 = 18$. Which number sentence is in the same fact family as $3 \times 6 = 18$?

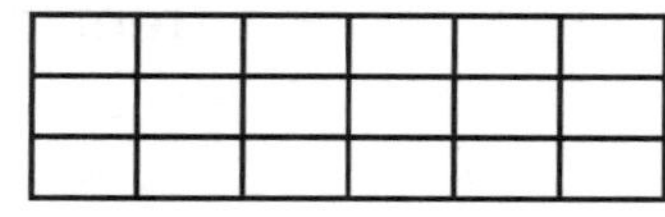

A $18 + 6 = 24$ Ⓐ
B $18 - 6 = 12$ Ⓑ
C $6 \times 3 = 18$ Ⓒ
D $18 \div 2 = 9$ Ⓓ

Relating Multiplication and Division as Arrays

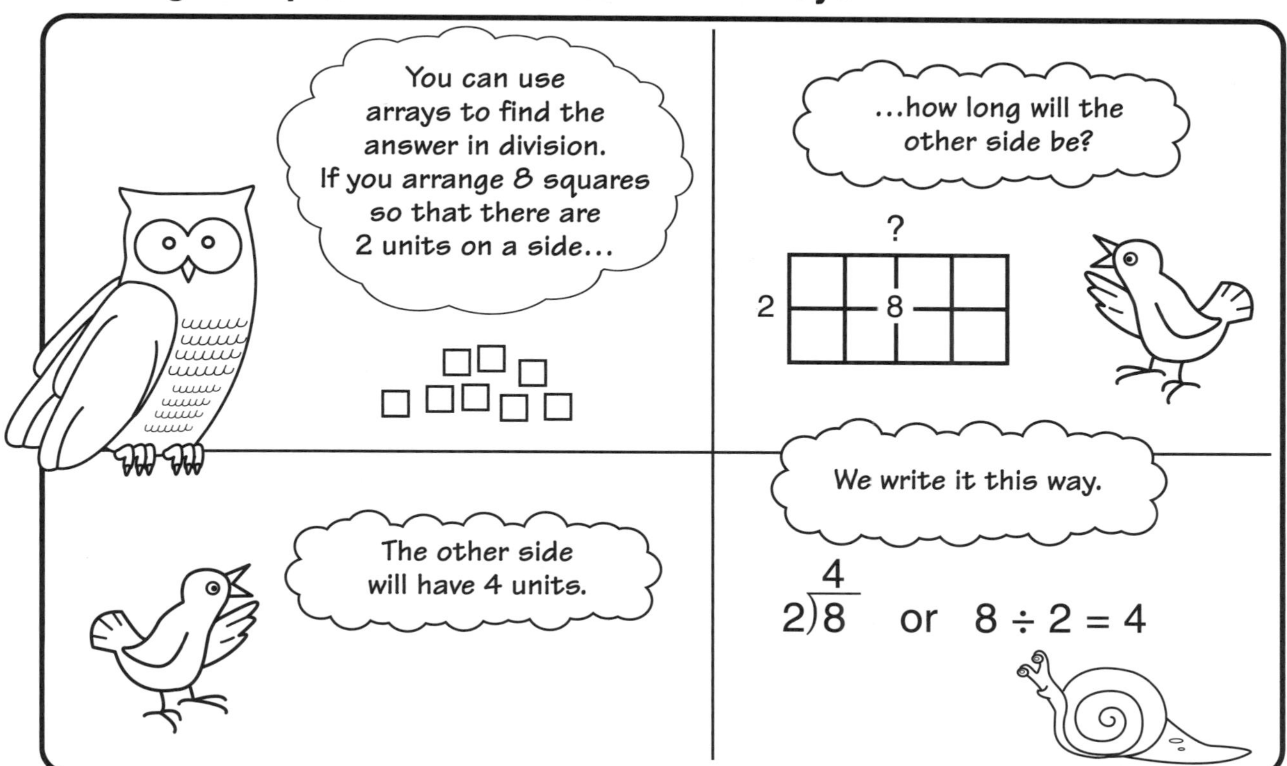

Use blocks or squares to find the missing side. Write a division fact.

1. Use 30 blocks with 5 units on one side. Missing side = ______

Division Fact: ____________________

2. Use 12 blocks with 2 units on one side. Missing side = ______

Division Fact: ____________________

3. Use 12 blocks with 3 units on one side. Missing side = ______

Division Fact: ____________________

4. Use 12 blocks with 4 units on one side. Missing side = ______

Division Fact: ____________________

How many units are on the missing side? Write the division fact in two ways.

5.

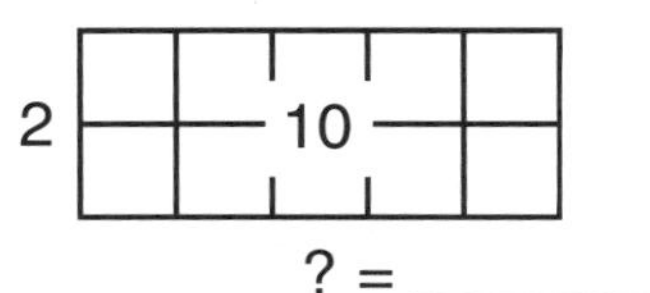

? = ________

__________ and __________

6.

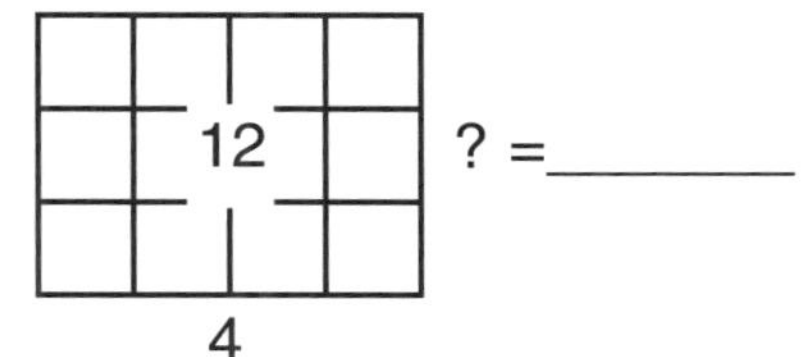

? = ________

__________ and __________

7. **You now know several different ways to find a quotient. How many different ways can you name?**

Finding the Cost Per Unit

Will bought 4 animal cards for 12¢.
Each card cost the same amount.
Find the cost of 1 card.

I could share 12¢ into 4 groups of equal size to find the cost of 1 card.

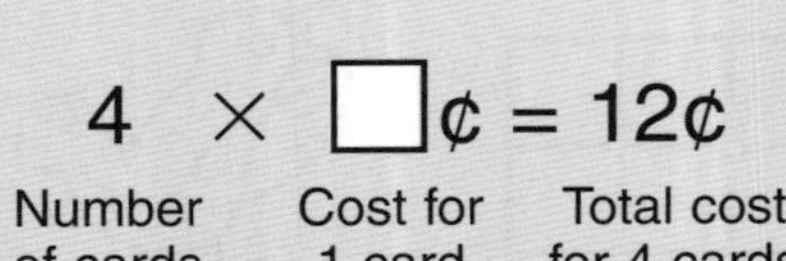

It will cost ______ pennies for each card.

12¢ ÷ 4 = ______¢ per unit.

Find the cost of one unit. Use cubes or pennies and paper plates for problems 1–3.

1. 3 × □¢ = 18¢
□ = ________¢

2. 4 × □¢ = 28¢
□ = ________¢

3. 5 × □¢ = 30¢
□ = ________¢

4. 2 × □¢ = 18¢
□ = ________¢

5. 3 × □¢ = 24¢
□ = ________¢

6. 4 × □¢ = 36¢
□ = ________¢

Write a number sentence using □ for the cost of 1 item. Find □.

7. A package of 3 crackers costs 15¢. Find the cost of one cracker.

□ = ________¢

8. A pack of 4 trading cards costs 36¢. Find the cost of one trading card.

No. sentence: ×□¢ = ¢

□ = ________¢

9. A package of 6 mini muffins costs 30¢. A package of 3 mini muffins costs 27¢. Which is the better buy? Explain.

____

____

____

10. A 3 pack of apple crisps costs 24¢. A 2 pack of apple crisps costs 18¢. Which is the better buy? Explain.

____

____

____

$n=?$

Problem Solving: Decide on a Process

1. Read and understand.
2. Find the question and needed facts.
3. Decide on a process.

Phil lives on a farm. He helps his family grow vegetables and fruits. They sell them at a roadside stand. On Saturday, Phil sold 12 baskets of apples for $3 a basket. How much money did the family earn?

Underline the question. Circle each fact.

What is the action in this problem? We are putting groups of the same size together ... this is multiplication.

$3 \times 12 = \square$

Answer: ____

Multiply 3 by the digit in the ones place.
Multiply 3 by the digit in the tens place.

Read. Tell the story to a partner. Underline the question. Circle the facts. Decide on the process. Choose the correct number sentence. Solve.

1. Dick's sister planted 8 rows of corn with 10 seeds in each row. How many corn seeds did she plant?

______

A $8 + 10 = \square$ **C** $10 \times 8 = \square$
B $10 - 8 = \square$ **D** $10 \div 8 = \square$

2. Jane got paid $3 for each bushel of corn she picked. If she earned $15, how many bushels of corn did she pick?

______

A $15 + 3 = \square$ **C** $15 \times 3 = \square$
B $15 - 3 = \square$ **D** $15 \div 3 = \square$

3. Rick picked 15 cartons of green beans. His sister picked 20 cartons of green beans. How many more cartons of green beans did his sister pick?

______

A $20 + 15 = \square$ **C** $20 \times 15 = \square$
B $20 - 15 = \square$ **D** $20 \div 15 = \square$

4. The family sold $400 of fruits and vegetables on Saturday and $200 on Sunday. How much did they sell both days?

______

A $400 + 200 = \square$ **C** $400 \times 200 = \square$
B $400 - 200 = \square$ **D** $400 \div 200 = \square$

Jill's cousin works 20 hours per week. He earns $5 per hour. How much does he earn in one week? Solve the problem and explain how you know what process to use.

Different Ways To Divide by 6

You have learned different ways to find a quotient.

The bagel shop sells bagels in bags of 6. John has 36 plain bagels to put in bags. How many bags does he need?

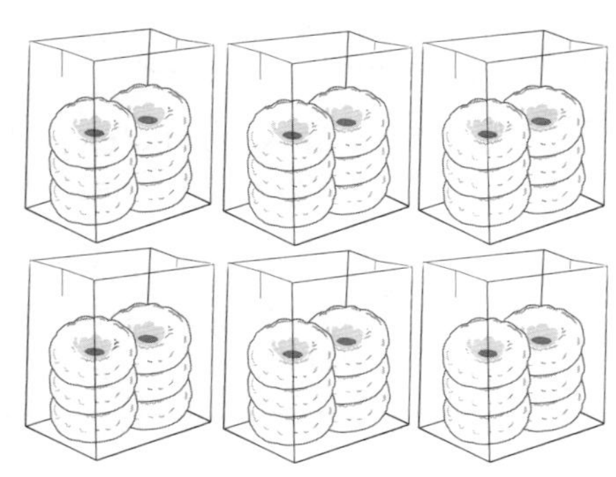

We could draw Xs and circle groups of 6 ...

☐ groups of 6 = 36

... or we could think of a missing factor.

$6 \times \square = 36$

$\square$ = ____ bags

1. Tisha has 48 salt bagels to put in bags. How many bags will Tisha need? ____

2. Maria has 42 raisin bagels to put in bags. How many bags will Maria need? ____

3. **Skip count backward by 6 from 54 to 0. Start at 54 and write each landing point. How many skips backward? ________ So 54 ÷ 6 = ________**

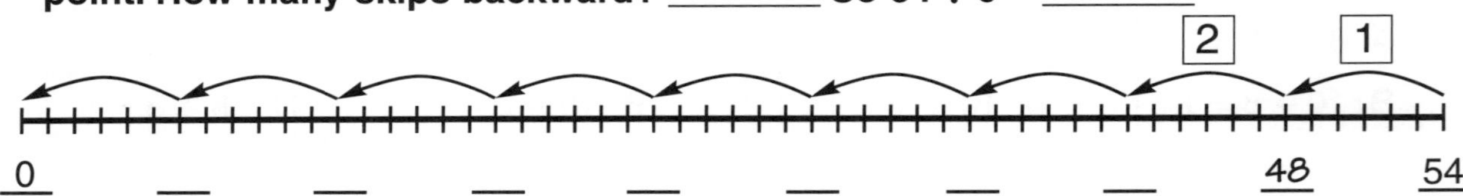

4. Use the multiplication table to divide by finding the missing factor.

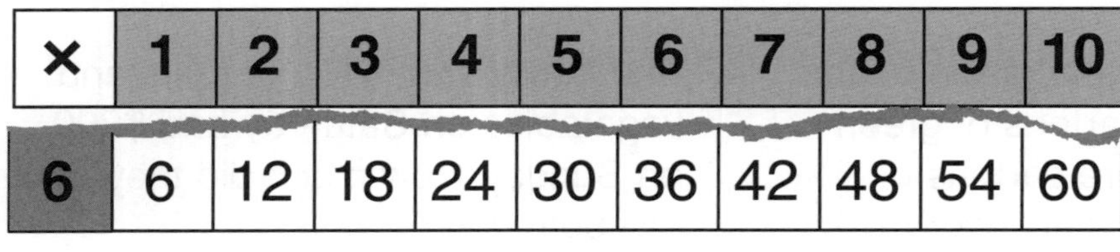

×	1	2	3	4	5	6	7	8	9	10
6	6	12	18	24	30	36	42	48	54	60

$6 \times \square = 36$ $\square$ = ____

$6 \times \square = 30$ $\square$ = ____

$6 \times \square = 54$ $\square$ = ____

$6 \times \square = 42$ $\square$ = ____

The force of gravity is 6 times greater on Earth than on the moon. If you weigh 60 pounds on Earth, you weigh 10 pounds on the moon.

5. A dog weighs 30 pounds on Earth. How much does the dog weigh on the moon? ____

6. A box of food weighs 24 pounds on Earth. How much does the food weigh on the moon? ____

Different Ways To Divide by 7

You have learned different ways to find a quotient.

Daria spends 56 hours a week sleeping. How many hours does Daria sleep in 1 day?

1 week has 7 days.
Think 7 × ☐ = 56.

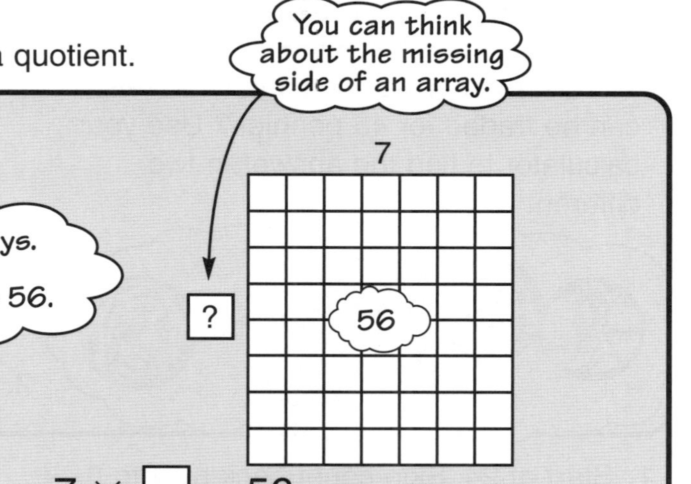

$7 \times \square = 56$

$\square$ = _____ hours a day

Find the quotient by finding the missing side of an array.

1. 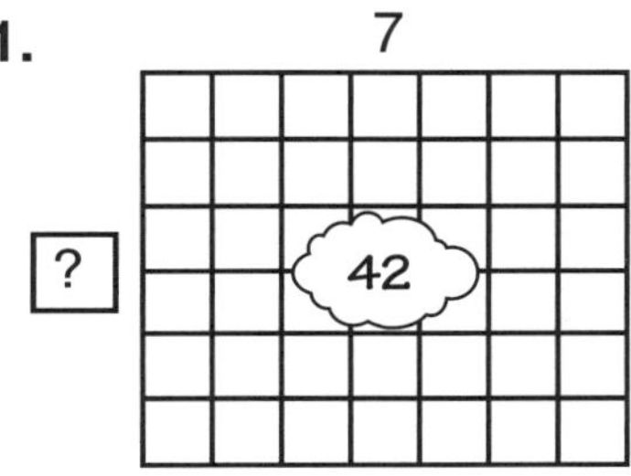

☐ × 7 = 42
☐ = _____

2. 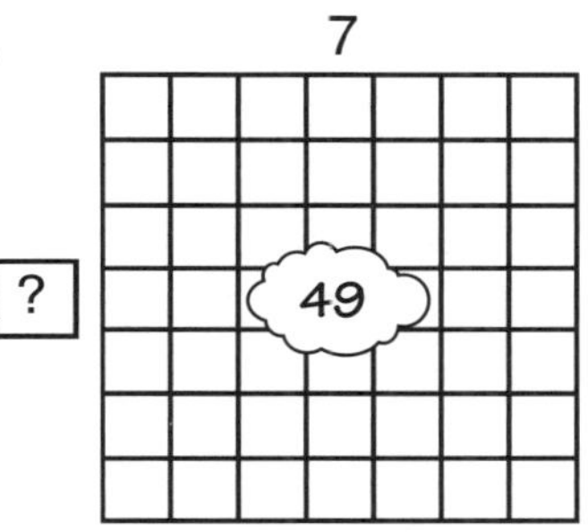

☐ × 7 = 49
☐ = _____

Use the multiplication table to divide by finding the missing factor.

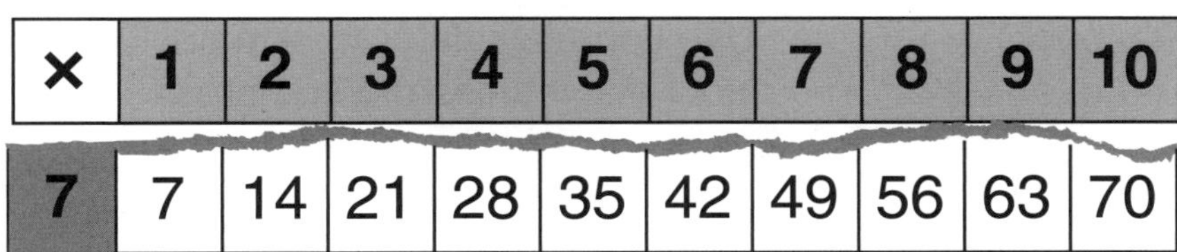

×	1	2	3	4	5	6	7	8	9	10
7	7	14	21	28	35	42	49	56	63	70

3. ☐ × 7 = 49   ☐ = _____   ☐ × 7 = 63   ☐ = _____

4. 7 × ☐ = 28   ☐ = _____   ☐ × 7 = 42   ☐ = _____

5. $42 \div 7 =$ _____ $56 \div 7 =$ _____ $7\overline{)35}$ $7\overline{)63}$ $7\overline{)49}$

6. **What 2 different ways are used to find the quotient on this page?**

Skip Counting Back on a Calculator

Jill has 45 pennies. How many nickels can be traded for 45 pennies? Use your calculator to find the answer in two different ways.

1. Enter [4] [5] [−] [5] [=].
   Keep pressing [=].
   How many total times must you press [=] to get 0? ______

2. Press [4] [5] [÷] [5] [=].

1. Start at 24. Skip count back by 4 to 0.

0 1 2 3 4 5 6 7 8 9 10 11 12 13 14 15 16 17 18 19 20 21 22 23 24

Use your calculator to skip count back by 4 from 24 to 0.

What keys do you press? ____ ____ ____ ____ ____ ____ ____ ____ ____ ____

How many times did you press [=]? ______

2. Use your calculator. Skip count back by 6 from 42 to 0. How many times did you press [=]? ______

3. Use your calculator. Skip count back by 7 from 56 to 0. How many times did you press [=]? ______

4. How many groups of 8 are in 72? Use your calculator to skip back. How many times did you press [=]? ______

5. How many groups of 9 are in 54? Use your calculator to skip back. How many times did you press [=]? ______

6. Skip count by 2 from 12 to 0 on your calculator. How many times did you press [=]? ______

7. Skip count by 3 from 36 to 0. How many times did you press [=]? ______

8. Skip count by 4 from 48 to 0. How many times did you press [=]? ______

9. Skip count by 5 from 100 to 0. How many times did you press [=]? ______

Dividing by 8

You have learned different ways to find a quotient.

There are 40 members of the swim team going to a swim meet. An equal number of members will be in each of 8 vans. How many members will be in each van?

I can subtract groups of 8.

$$\begin{array}{r}40\\-8\\\hline32\end{array}\quad\begin{array}{r}32\\-8\\\hline24\end{array}\quad\begin{array}{r}24\\-8\\\hline16\end{array}\quad\begin{array}{r}16\\-8\\\hline8\end{array}\quad\begin{array}{r}8\\-8\\\hline0\end{array}$$

I can use counters or draw pictures with an equal number in each van.

I can think of the related multiplication fact.

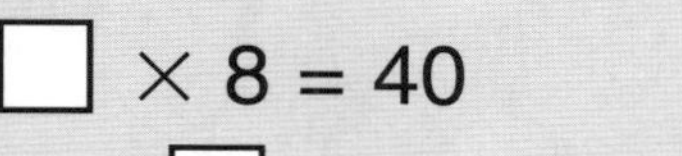

□ × 8 = 40

□ = _____ members

1. Use the number line to write a multiplication fact and a related division fact for 3, 8, and 24.

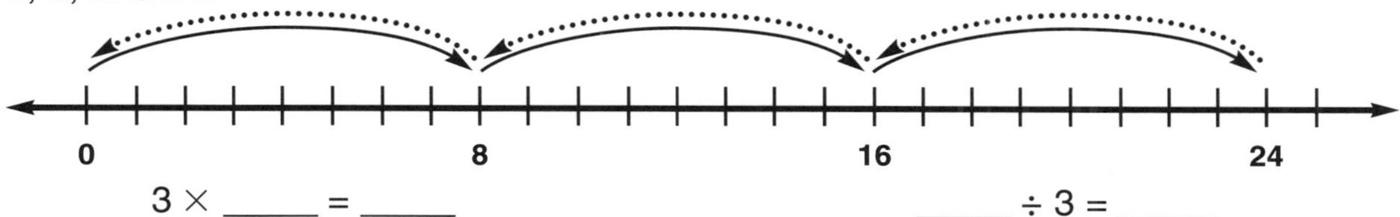

3 × _____ = _____   _____ ÷ 3 = _____

Write a division fact and a multiplication fact for each array.

2. _____ ÷ 8 = _____

   _____ × 8 = _____

3. 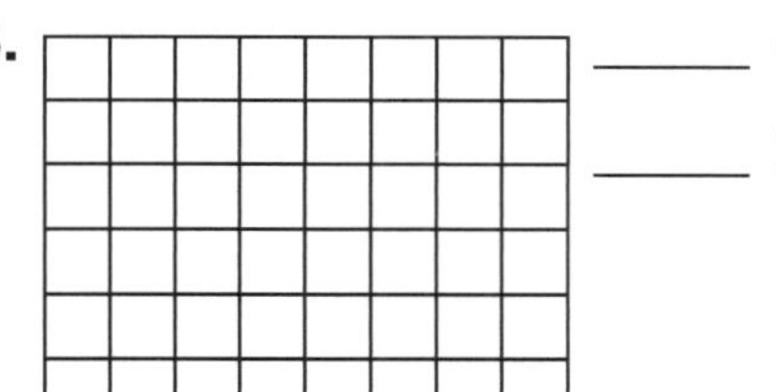

   _____ ÷ 8 = _____

   _____ × 8 = _____

Solve.

4. $8\overline{)40}$

5. 8 × □ = 56

6. 8 × □ = 72

7. Raymond divides 48 Cheesie Crackers among 8 friends. How many crackers does each friend get? _____

8. Pencils are on sale for 8¢ each. How many pencils could Maria buy with 64¢? _____

TEST PREP

Which number sentence is not related to the picture on the number line?

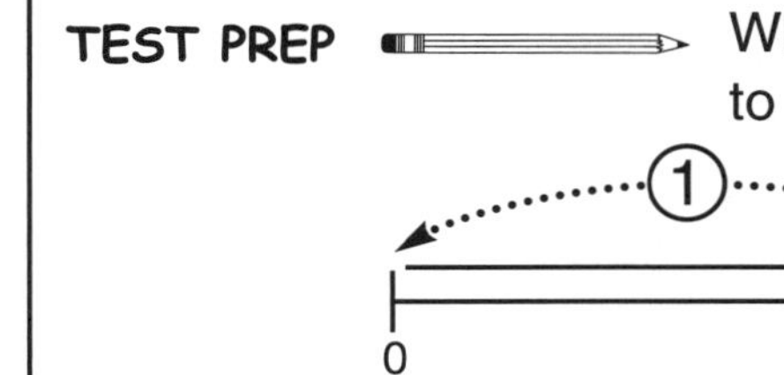

A 16 ÷ 8 = 2 Ⓐ
B 16 ÷ 2 = 8 Ⓑ
C 8 ÷ 2 = 4 Ⓒ
D 2 × 8 = 16 Ⓓ

n=?

Dividing by 9

There are 9 players on a baseball team.
There are 54 players in the league.
How many teams are there in the league?

I can form an array with 9 in each row.

9

$\square \times 9 = 54,$

$\square$ = _____ teams

1. Complete the table of multiples of 9.

1	2	3	4	5	6	7	8	9	10
9	18								90

Write two multiplication facts and two division facts for each array.

2.

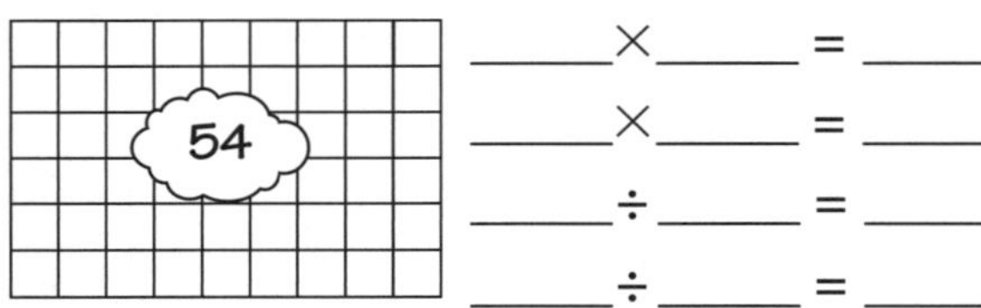

_____ × _____ = _____
_____ × _____ = _____
_____ ÷ _____ = _____
_____ ÷ _____ = _____

3.

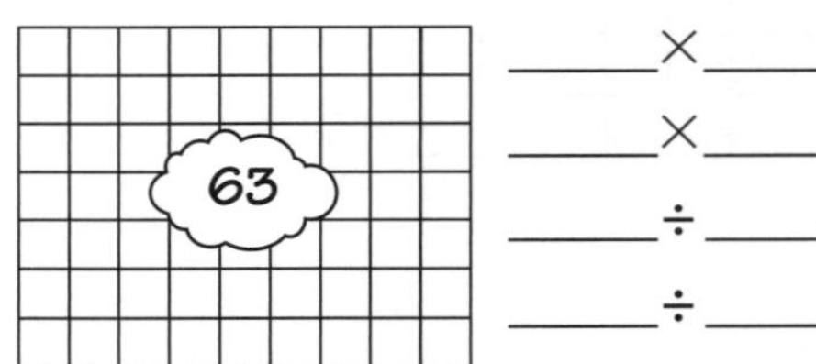

_____ × _____ = _____
_____ × _____ = _____
_____ ÷ _____ = _____
_____ ÷ _____ = _____

4. $9\overline{)63}$ $9\overline{)45}$ $9\overline{)81}$ $9\overline{)54}$ $9\overline{)72}$ $9\overline{)36}$

5. Tickets are sold for the baseball games in sets of 9. If you want to buy 36 tickets, how many sets should you buy?

_____

6. John had 54 baseball cards. If he and 8 friends share the cards equally, how many cards will each receive?

_____

Different Ways To Divide

You have learned different ways to find a quotient. Each way is related to one of the ways you learned multiplication facts. Here are different ways to find the quotient of 12 ÷ 3.

Method A

Share equally onto 3 plates.

Method B

Sorting groups of 3.
Circle groups of 3.

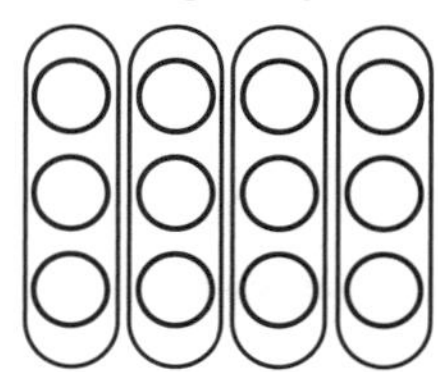

Method C

Subtracting equal groups.

$$\begin{array}{r} 12 \\ -\ 3 \\ \hline 9 \end{array} \rightarrow \begin{array}{r} 9 \\ -\ 3 \\ \hline 6 \end{array} \rightarrow \begin{array}{r} 6 \\ -\ 3 \\ \hline 3 \end{array} \rightarrow \begin{array}{r} 3 \\ -\ 3 \\ \hline 0 \end{array}$$

Method D

Skip count backwards
on a number line.

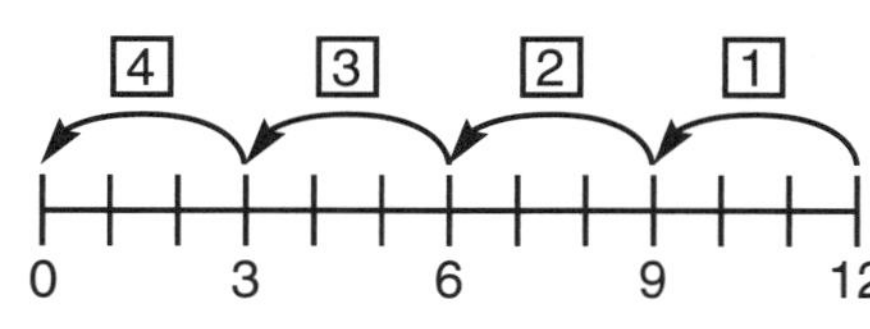

Method E

Find the missing
side of an array.

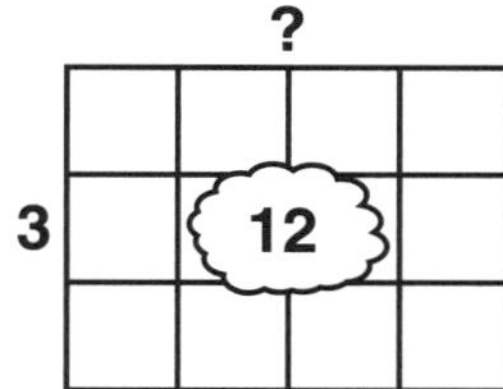

Method F

Find the missing factor in a
related multiplication fact.

$$3 \times \square = 12$$

Find the quotient. Try to use each method once.

1. You cut strips of ribbon that are 4 feet long from a 12-foot roll. How many strips do you have?

   Method _______ Quotient _______

2. You pack 3 tennis balls into each can. How many cans do you fill with 18 balls?

   Method _______ Quotient _______

3. You live 12 blocks from school. You rest every 3 blocks on your walk home. How many rests will you take?

   Method _______ Quotient _______

4. You pack 15 pieces of candy into a box. You put an equal number into each of 3 rows. How many pieces are in each row?

   Method _______ Quotient _______

5. You share 15 apples with 3 friends. How many apples does each friend receive?

   Method _______ Quotient _______

6. You know your multiplication facts. You want to divide 27 by 3.

   Method _______ Quotient _______

Sharing, with Leftovers

There are 4 friends sharing 13 crackers.
How many crackers will each friend get?

Use 5 small plates and 20 counters, such as buttons, cubes, or beans. Share. Complete the chart.

	Number of Counters	Number of Plates	How many on each?	Remainder?	Fact
	7	2	3	1	$2\overline{)7}$ 3 R1
1.	18	4			
2.	14	4			
3.	9	2			
4.	12	5			
5.	14	3			
6.	17	3			
7.	18	5			
8.	19	4			

TEST PREP

$4\overline{)14}$

A 3 Ⓐ
B 3 R2 Ⓑ
C 3 R4 Ⓒ
D 5 Ⓓ

Using a Multiplication Table To Divide

You can use a multiplication table to divide.

You have 21¢. You want to buy marbles that cost 4¢ each. How many marbles can you buy?

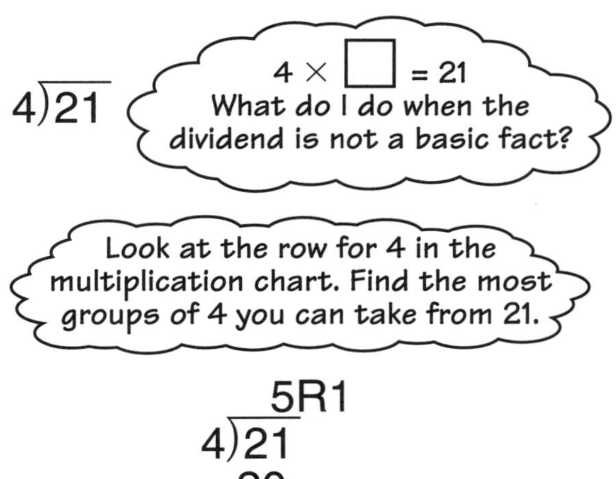

$$\begin{array}{r} 5\text{R}1 \\ 4\overline{)21} \\ \underline{20} \\ 1 \end{array}$$

×	1	2	3	4	5	6	7	8	9
1	1	2	3	4	5	6	7	8	9
2	2	4	6	8	10	12	14	16	18
3	3	6	9	12	15	18	21	24	27
4	4	8	12	16	20	24	28	32	36
5	5	10	15	20	25	30	35	40	45
6	6	12	18	24	30	36	42	48	54
7	7	14	21	28	35	42	49	56	63
8	8	16	24	32	40	48	56	64	72
9	9	18	27	36	45	54	63	72	81

You can buy _______ marbles and will have _______ ¢ left.

Use your multiplication table to divide.

1. $4\overline{)9}$ R $\qquad 4\overline{)25}$ R $\qquad 4\overline{)14}$ R $\qquad 8\overline{)19}$ R

2. $6\overline{)14}$ R $\qquad 6\overline{)25}$ R $\qquad 7\overline{)38}$ R $\qquad 7\overline{)44}$ R

3. Carol had 40¢. Cookies cost 6¢ each. How many cookies can Carol buy and how much money will she have left? _________ _________

4. Ramon had 50¢. Cookies cost 6¢ each. How many cookies can Ramon buy and how much money will he have left? _________ _________

5. Pencils cost 6¢. How many pencils can Dick buy with 50¢ and how much money will he have left? _________ _________

6. Mini muffins cost 9¢ each. How many mini muffins can Mike buy with 60¢ and how much money will he have left? _________ _________

Reasonable Answers Involving Remainders

In word problems, remainders are very important. They can change your final answer.

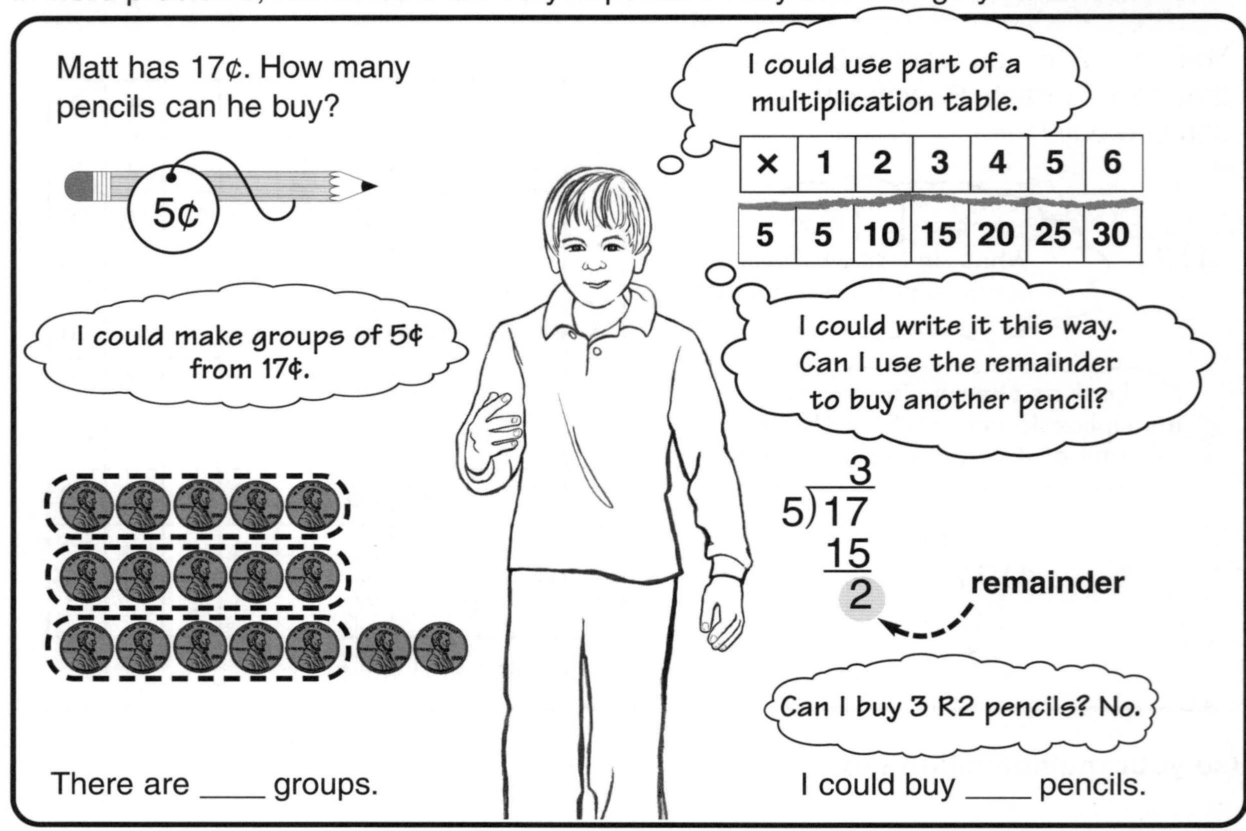

Study the remainder carefully to answer each question.

1. A pencil box holds 6 pencils. How many boxes are needed to hold 16 pencils? ________

2. A notepad costs 4¢. How many notepads can be bought with 15¢? ________

3. You can put 5 bagels in a bag. How many bags will you need for 32 bagels? ________

4. A colored pencil costs 7¢. How many colored pencils can be bought with 25¢? ________

5. A can holds 3 tennis balls. How many cans are needed to hold 23 balls? ________

6. A brownie recipe calls for 2 eggs. Kate has 7 eggs. How many batches of brownies can she make? ________

7. Each shelf is 2 feet long. How many shelves can be cut from a 9-foot board? ________

8. Each table seats 4 students. How many tables are needed to seat 29 students? ________

Drawing Pictures To Divide

You can draw pictures to divide with base ten blocks. Use | for tens and • for ones.

There are 46 students on the playground. The teacher separates them into 2 groups of equal size. How many students are in each group?

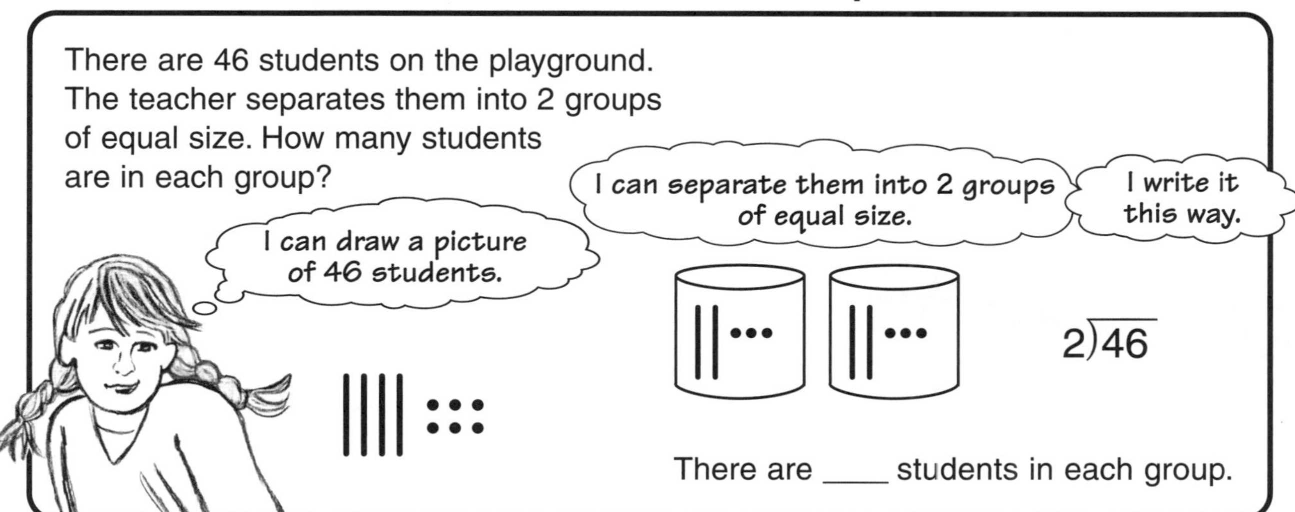

There are ____ students in each group.

	Start with	Divide into groups of equal size	Write this way
1.	||| ||| •••	3 groups: ||• ||• ||•	21 over 3)63
2.	||| ||| ••••••	3 groups	)
3.	|||| |||| ••••	4 groups	)
4.	5)55	5 groups	)
5.	4)40	4 groups	)
6.	4)80	4 groups	)

2-Digit Dividends

A class of 36 students is going on a field trip in 3 vans. How many students will ride in each van?

3)36

Build 36 (36 = 3 tens and 6 ones). Share tens and ones among 3 plates.

Each plate will have 1 ten and 2 ones.

12 students
3)36

Build and share using base ten blocks.

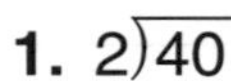

1. 2)40 **2.** 3)60 **3.** 80 ÷ 4 = ☐ **4.** 90 ÷ 3 = ☐

5. 2)66 **6.** 2)46 **7.** 5)55 **8.** 2)42

9. 3)63 **10.** 3)36 **11.** 3)96 **12.** 2)60

13. There are 8 cakes to be shared equally among 80 people. Into how many pieces should each cake be cut?

______

14. There are 96 pencils. Each bag gets 3 pencils. How many bags are needed?

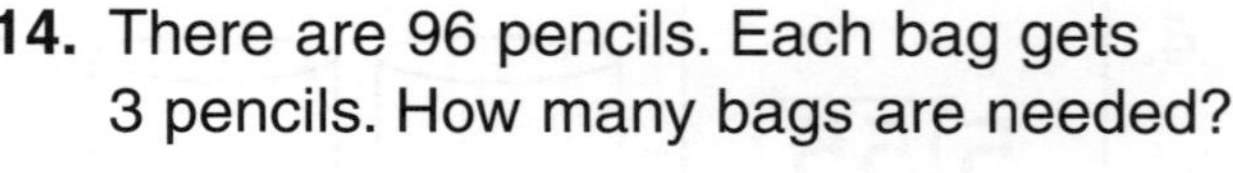

______

TEST PREP

3)69

A 20 Ⓐ
B 20 R9 Ⓑ
C 23 Ⓒ
D 209 Ⓓ

Checking Multiplication and Division

Multiplication and division are opposite or inverse operations. You can use division to check multiplication. You can use multiplication to check division.

There are 2 cupcakes in a package. How many cupcakes are in 23 packages?

Solve: $23 \times 2 = 46$ ⟷ should be the same ⟷ **Check:** $2\overline{)46}$

There are 63 cans of juice. They are put in packages of 3. How many packages are there?

$3\overline{)63}$ = 21 ⟷ should be the same ⟷ 21×3

Yumi Juice

Find the product. Check by dividing.

1. 31×2 **Check:**

2. 21×3 **Check:**

Find the quotient. Check by multiplying.

3. $4\overline{)44}$ **Check:**

4. $3\overline{)36}$ **Check:**

Estimate. Solve. Check by using the opposite operation.

	Estimate	Solve	Check
5. The cook bought 4 dozen eggs for breakfast. How many eggs did the cook buy?			
6. Mark packs 50 balloons for a school carnival. He puts 5 balloons into each small bag. How many bags will he pack?			

Using a Model To Discover Division Patterns

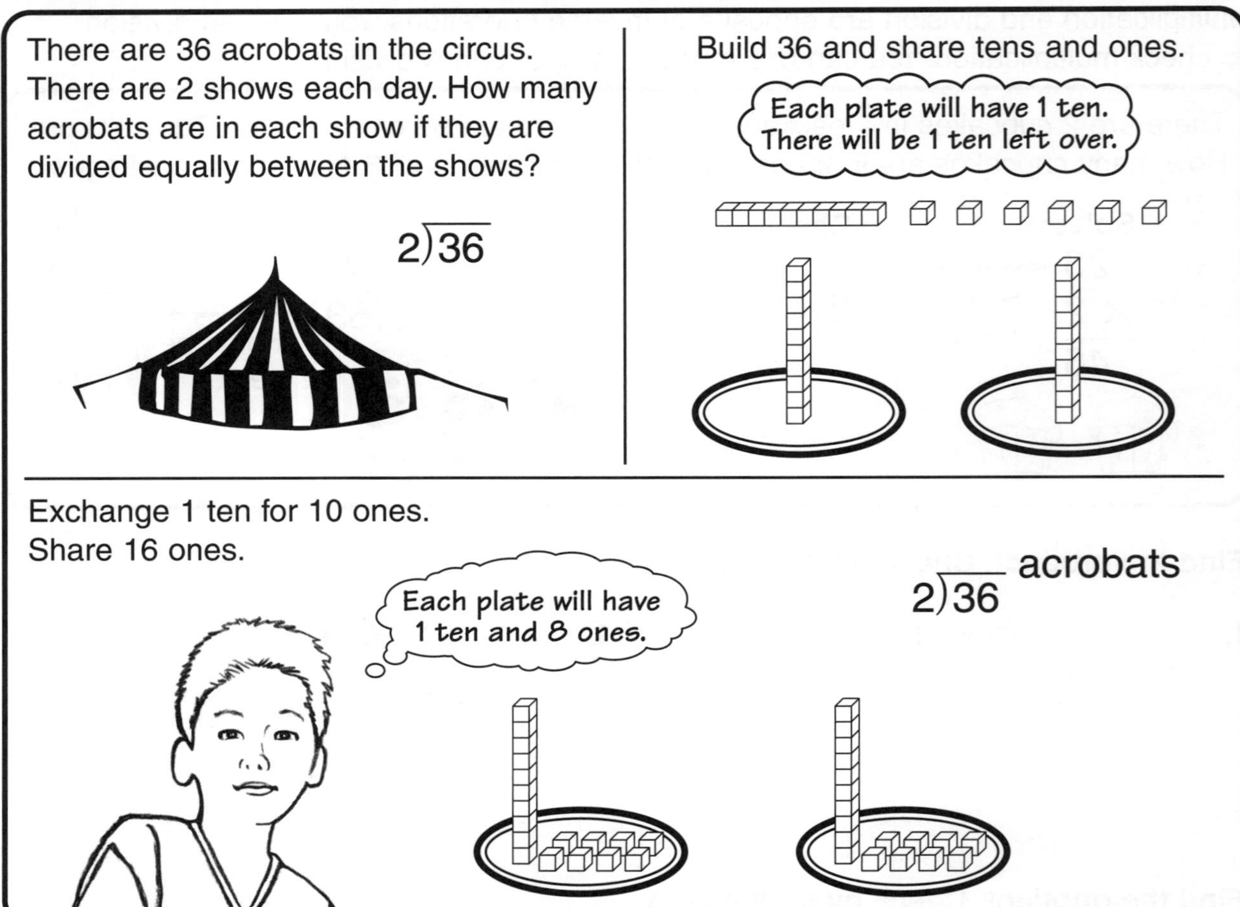

Build and share base ten blocks. Record the answer.

1. 4)52 **2.** 5)75 **3.** 3)78 **4.** 7)84

5. 3)75 **6.** 4)96 **7.** 7)91 **8.** 8)96

9. Tammy read a 65-page book in 5 days. She read the same number of pages each day. How many pages did she read each day? ________

10. There are 72 students in the 3 classrooms of the fourth grade. If each classroom has the same number of students, how many students are in each room? ________

Finding Steps in Long Division by Dividing with Blocks

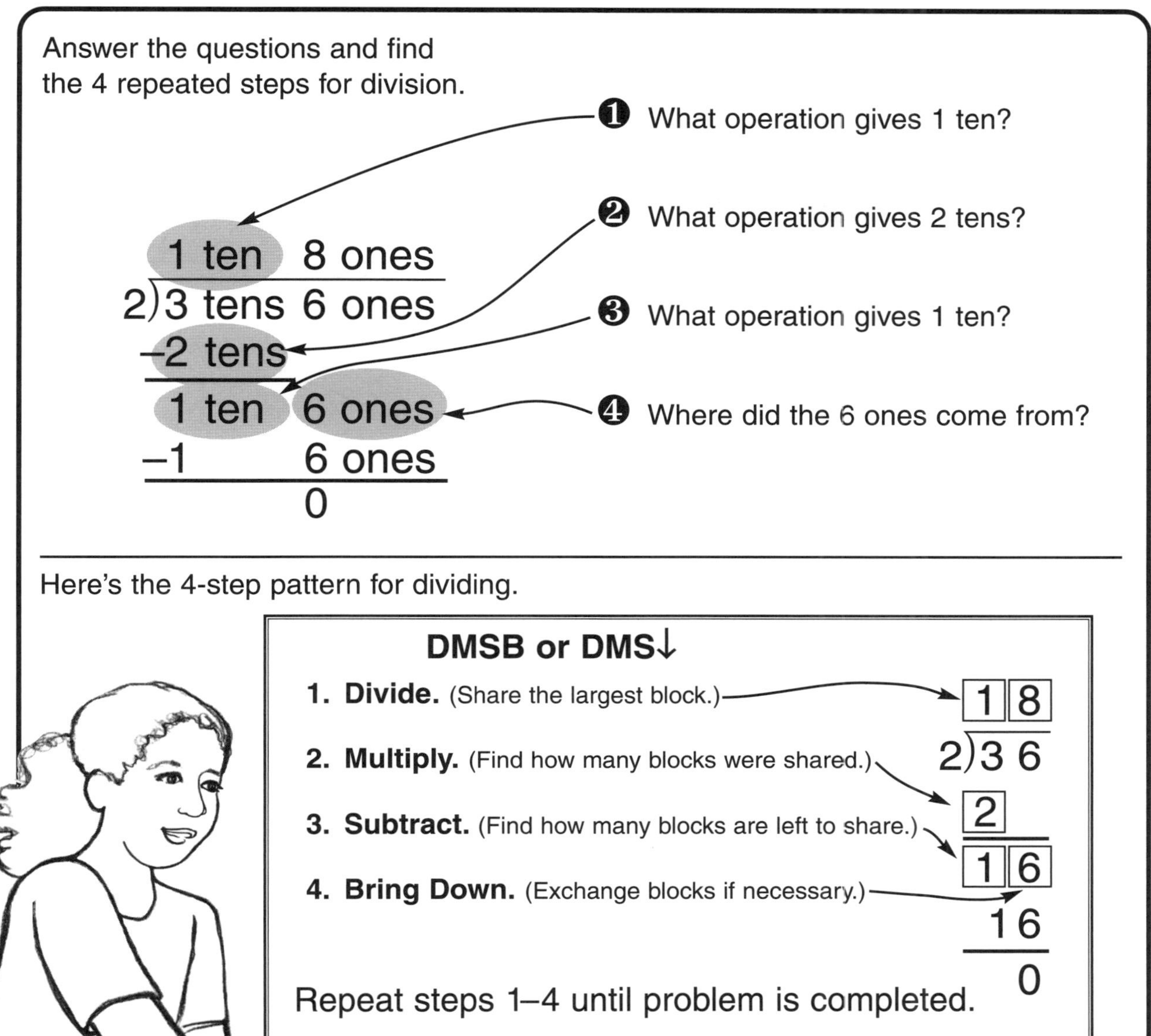

Use the 4-step pattern to divide. Use base ten blocks to check your answer.

1. 4)64 = 16 (4, 24, 24, 0)

2. 5)85

3. 3)87

4. 7)84

5. 6)72

6. 5)65

7. 8)92

8. 7)78

Drawing Pictures To Divide

You can draw a picture to record what you do with base ten blocks.

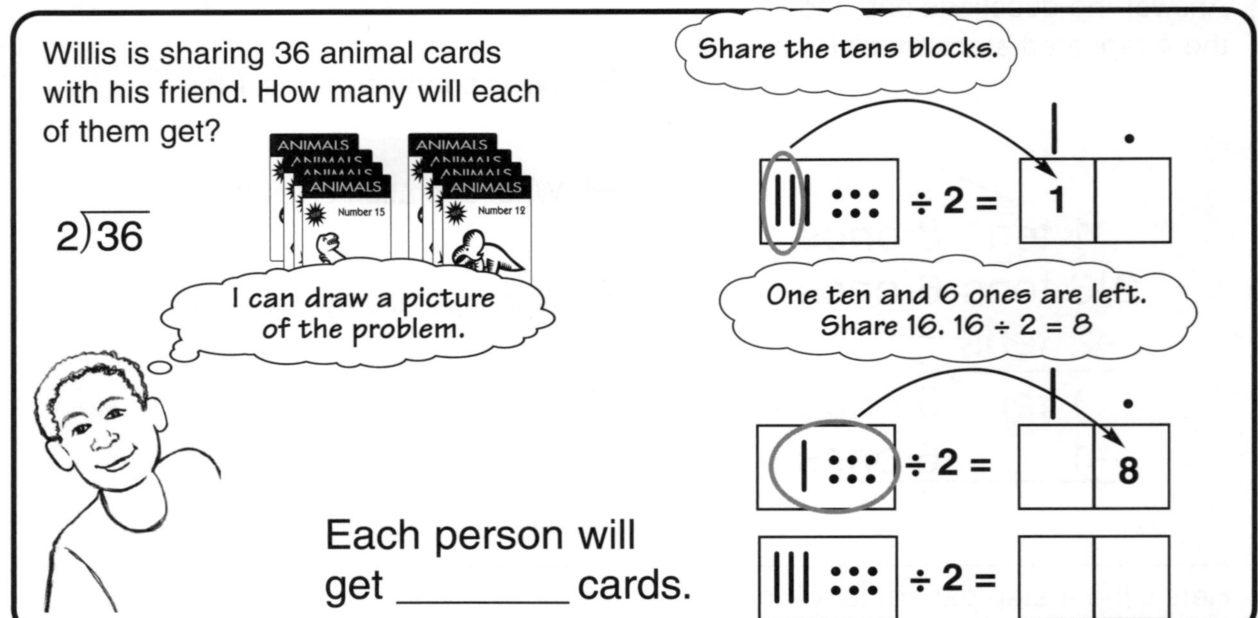

Draw pictures to divide. Use mental math to share the ones.

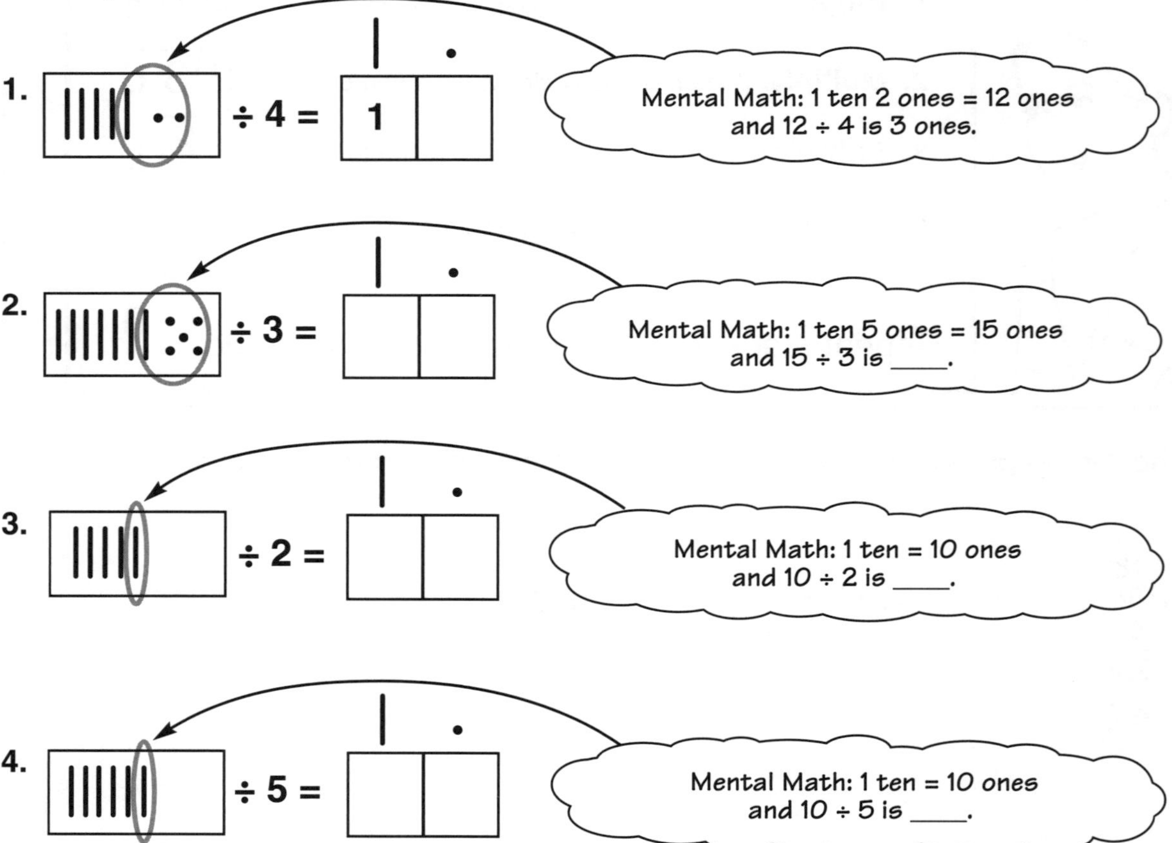

Draw the number 72 with pictures of base ten blocks. Next use the pictures to divide 72 by 3. Explain why you need to exchange 1 ten for 10 ones.

Finding the Mean or Average

The mean or average is the sum of the numbers in a set divided by the number of numbers in the set. The numbers are evened out so they are all the same.

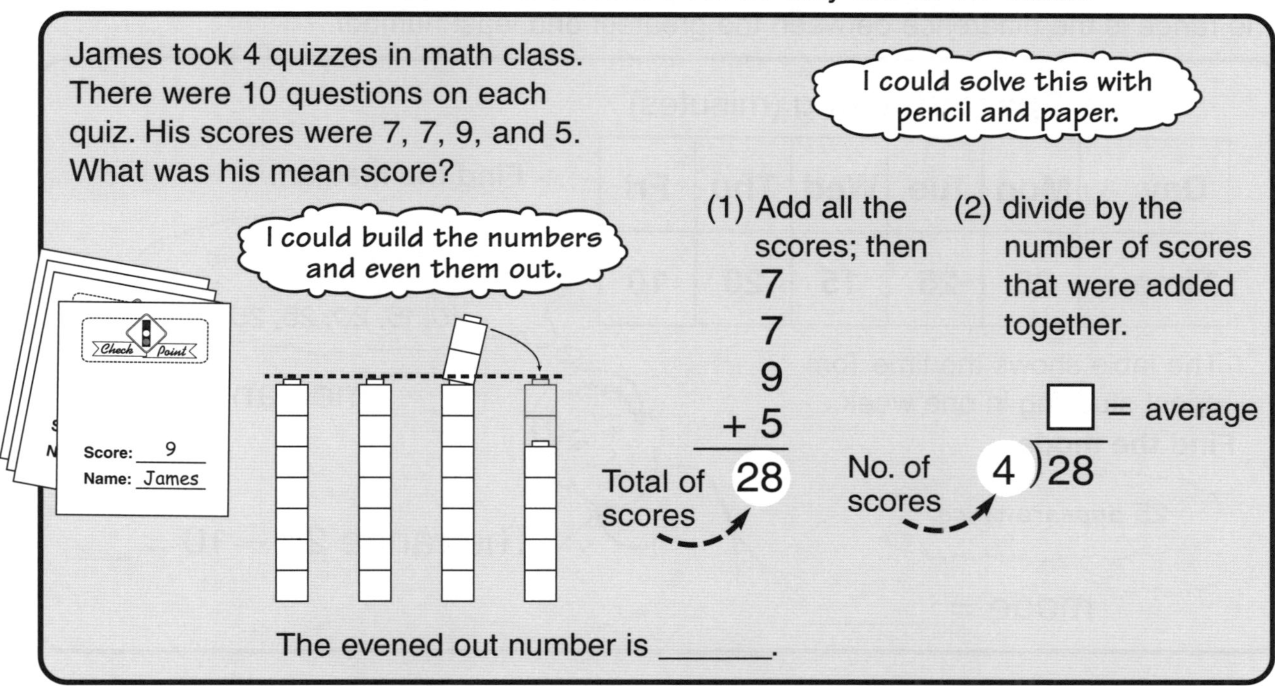

Follow two steps to find the mean score for each group.

1. On 3 quizzes Rochelle's scores were 7, 5, and 6. What is her average score? ______

2. On 5 quizzes Trevor's scores were 6, 9, 8, 7, and 10. What is his mean score? ______

3. On 4 quizzes Kelsey's scores were 4, 7, 5, and 8. Find her average score. ______

4. On 5 quizzes Patrick's scores were 4, 5, 6, 7, and 8. Find his mean score. ______

5. On 4 quizzes Chanise's scores were 8, 9, 7, and 4. Find her average score. ______

6. On 3 quizzes Winton's scores were 7, 8, and 6. Find his mean score. ______

TEST PREP

Find the mean of these numbers: 8, 9, 5, and 6

A 6 Ⓐ
B 7 Ⓑ
C 8 Ⓒ
D 28 Ⓓ

Mode, Median and Range

The mode is the number that you see most often in a set of numbers. The median of the set is the middle number when the numbers are in order from least to greatest. The range is the difference between the greatest and least number.

Time Spent Studying (minutes)

Day	Mon	Tue	Wed	Thu	Fri
Time	25	25	15	20	10

The table shows the time Tom spent studying in one week.

Find the mode.

25 appears twice.

mode = ______

Find the median.

Write the numbers in order:
10, 15, 20, 25, 25

median = ______

The range 25 – 10 = ___

1. Find the median for the weekly allowances:

$12, $5, $10, $15, $8

median = ________

2. Find the median for the high temperatures for five days:

60°, 54°, 48°, 64°, 52°

median = ________

3. The table shows the test scores for the class.

Score	Number of students
96%	|
90%	||
84%	||||
70%	|||

Mode?________

Range?________

4. The graph shows the number of books read by five students.

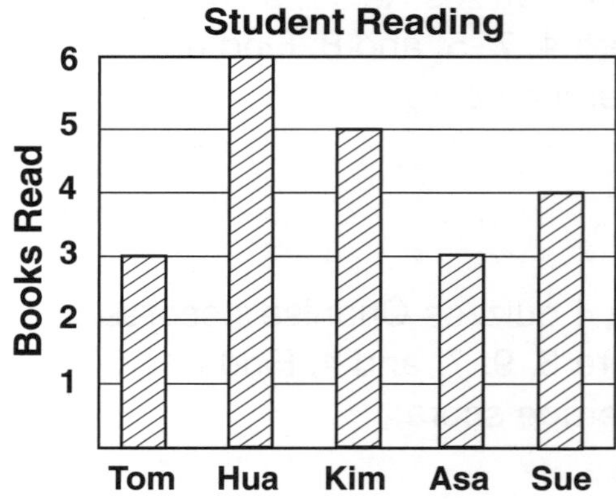

Mode?________

Median?________

3-Digit Dividends

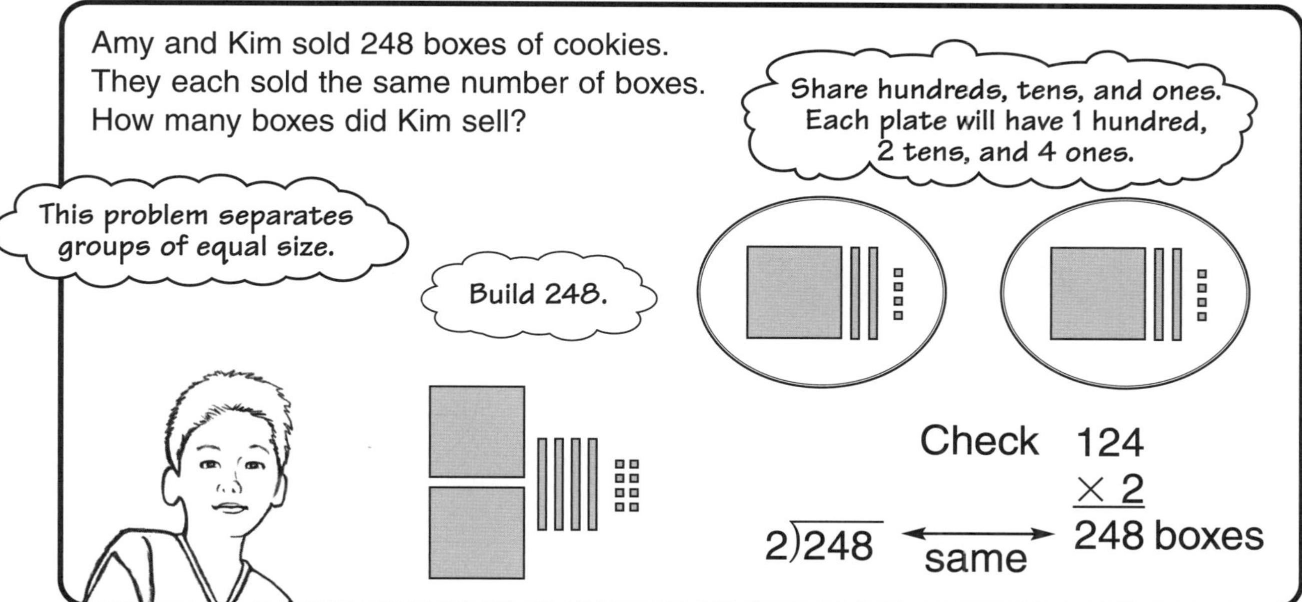

Share base ten blocks. Check by multiplying.

1. $2\overline{)424}$ Check:

2. $2\overline{)682}$ Check:

3. $2\overline{)668}$ Check:

Find the quotients. Check with base ten blocks.

4. $5\overline{)500}$

5. $3\overline{)960}$

6. $2\overline{)480}$

7. In *Narrative of the Life of Frederick Douglass*, Frederick escapes to freedom. If he traveled 108 miles in 9 hours, how many miles did he travel each hour?

____

8. Mrs. Auld teaches Frederick to write his ABCs. If Frederick used 228 letters to practice writing 4-letter words, how many words did he write?

____

TEST PREP

$4\overline{)480}$

- **A** 12 Ⓐ
- **B** 100 Ⓑ
- **C** 102 Ⓒ
- **D** 120 Ⓓ

Dividing a 3-Digit Number with Regrouping

Find the quotients.

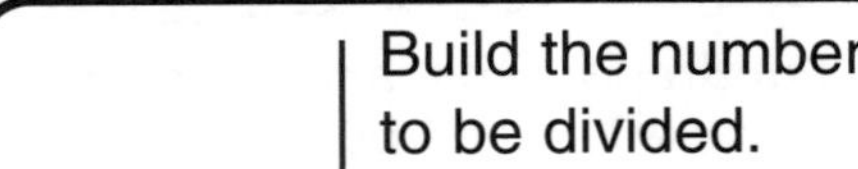

$3\overline{)436}$

Build the number to be divided.

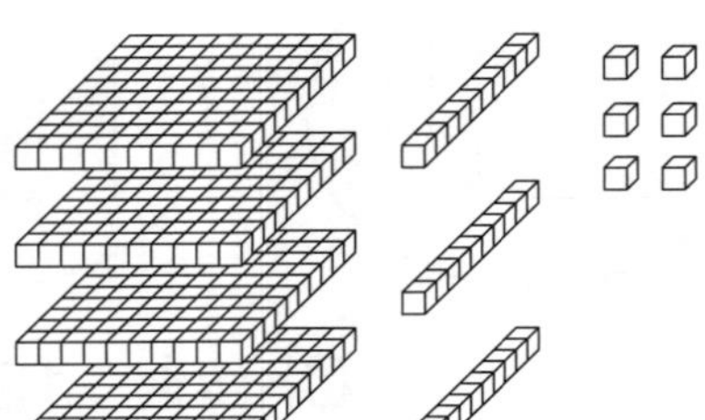

Share the hundreds.
(Exchange "leftovers" for smaller blocks.)
Share the tens.
(Exchange "leftovers" for smaller blocks.)
Share the ones.
(The "leftovers" become the remainder.)

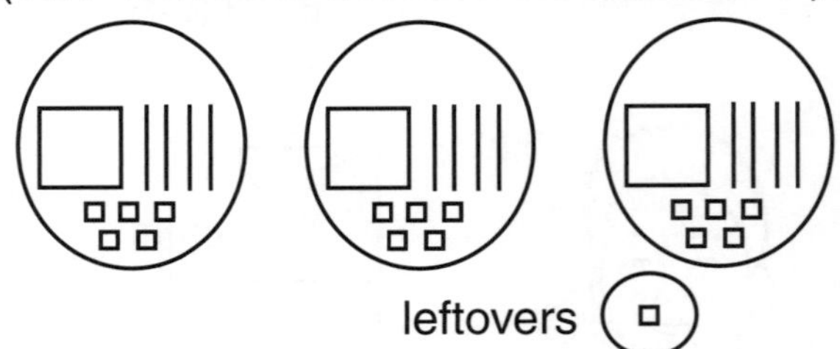

leftovers

Use the division recipe three times.

- **D** ... Divide
- **M** ... Multiply
- **S** ... Subtract
- ↓ ... Bring down

1. **DMS↓** (hundreds)

```
   1
3)436
  3
  13
```

2. **DMS↓** (tens)

```
   14
3)436
  3
  13
  12
   16
```

3. **DMS↓** (ones)

```
   145 R1
3)436
  3
  13
  12
   16
   15
    1
```

Divide.

1.	$2\overline{)534}$	**2.**	$3\overline{)462}$	**3.**	$4\overline{)512}$	**4.**	$5\overline{)765}$
5.	$4\overline{)933}$	**6.**	$3\overline{)609}$	**7.**	$7\overline{)940}$	**8.**	$6\overline{)608}$

9. Summer, Sara, and Jessica collected 140 pennies in a jar. If they share the pennies equally, how many pennies will each get? How many will be left over?

______ , ______

10. Jill has 346 sheets of colored paper. If she makes the sheets into 5 drawing books, how many sheets of paper will be in each book? How many sheets will be left over?

______ , ______

11.  **When you divide a 3-digit number, what are the four steps you do with each digit?**

Dividing by 1 Digit with Regrouping

Marian and Kim babysit together and share the money they earn. During January, the girls earned $136 for babysitting. What is each girl's fair share?

This problem separates a number into groups of equal size.

$2\overline{)136}$

Build 136.

Share hundreds. — 1 hundred cannot be shared. After exchanging 1 hundred for 10 tens, there are 13 tens.

Share tens. — Each plate receives 6 tens. 1 ten is exchanged for 10 ones, so there are 16 ones.

Share ones. — Each plate receives 8 ones.

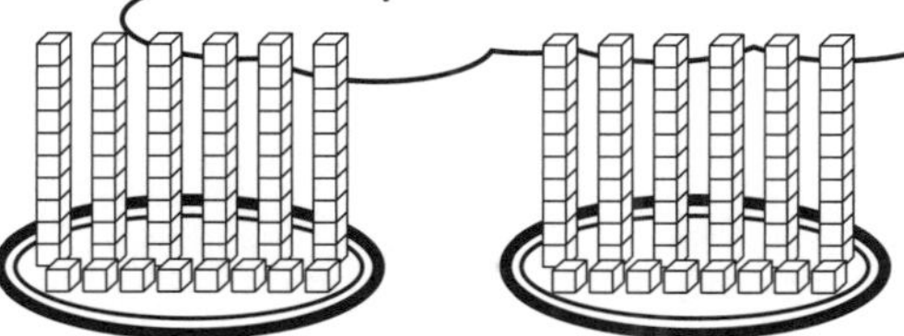

Use the division pattern **DMS↓** to record.

1. Share the hundreds. (In this problem, there are not enough hundreds to share, so move on to step 2.)

```
   0
2)1 3 6
  0
  1 3
```

2. Share the tens.

```
   0 6
2)1 3 6
  0
  1 3
  1 2
    1
```

3. Share the ones.

```
   0 6 8
2)1 3 6
  0
  1 3
  1 2
    1 6
    1 6
      0
```

$______ each

Use base ten blocks to divide. Use the pattern to record.

1. $2\overline{)158}$
2. $2\overline{)114}$
3. $2\overline{)168}$
4. $2\overline{)150}$
5. $3\overline{)135}$
6. $3\overline{)264}$
7. $3\overline{)162}$
8. $3\overline{)285}$
9. Danny needs to finish reading a book in 3 days. If the book is 150 pages long, how many pages should he read each day? ______
10. Rita's family plants a vegetable garden with 4 equal rows. If there are 128 plants in the garden, how many plants are in each row? ______

4-Digit Dividends

Joan's brother earned $2324 in 2 months. If he earned the same amount of money each month, how much did he earn in 1 month?

Taking a number apart into groups of equal size is division. Build the number with blocks. Share the blocks on 2 plates.

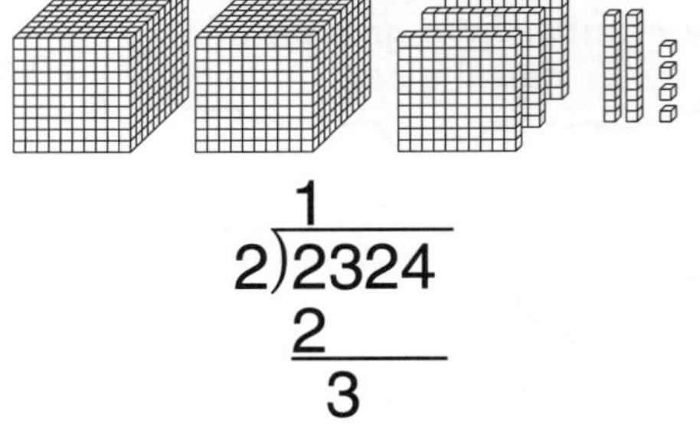

Each plate will get...

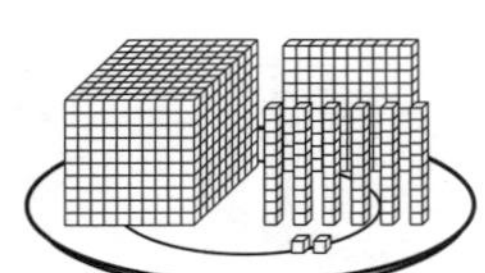

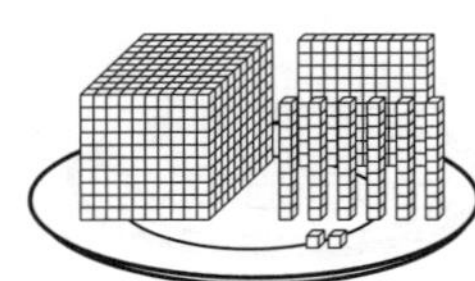

$$\begin{array}{r} 1 \\ 2\overline{)2324} \\ \underline{2} \\ 3 \end{array}$$

He earned $ ________

Share the blocks on paper plates. Record.

1. $2\overline{)2526}$

2. $2\overline{)2724}$

Use the four steps: DMS↓.

3. $4\overline{)8448}$

4. $3\overline{)8526}$

5. $5\overline{)6250}$

6. $3\overline{)9630}$

7. $6\overline{)6894}$

8. $7\overline{)8491}$

9. In gym class, groups of 4 students run a mile-long relay. A mile is 5280 feet. If they run equal distances, how many feet does each student run?

____

10. If groups of 3 students run equal distances in the relay, how many feet will each student run?

____

4-Digit Dividends

Mr. and Mrs. Traugot drove 1346 miles in 2 days. If they drove an equal number of miles each day, how many miles did they drive per day?

$2\overline{)1346}$

$$\begin{array}{r} 06 \\ 2\overline{)1346} \\ \underline{12} \\ 1 \end{array}$$

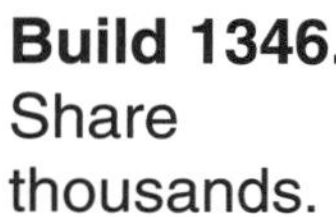

Build 1346.
Share thousands.

1 thousand must be exchanged for 10 hundreds, making a total of 13 hundreds.

Share hundreds.

There will be 6 hundreds on each plate. After 1 hundred is exchanged for 10 tens, there are 14 tens.

Share tens.

There will be 7 tens on each plate.

Share ones.

There will be 3 ones on each plate.

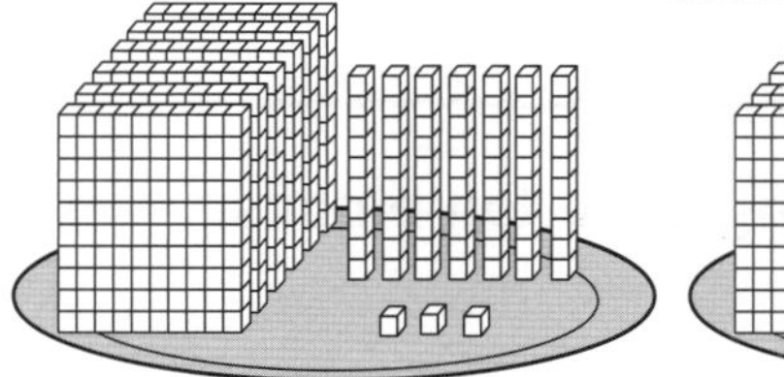

6 hundreds 7 tens 3 ones = ______ miles

Use base ten blocks to find the quotients.

1. $4\overline{)1820}$ **2.** $5\overline{)1180}$ **3.** $2\overline{)1534}$

Use the division pattern (DMS↓) to find the quotients.

4. $6\overline{)8244}$ **5.** $7\overline{)9184}$ **6.** $8\overline{)9232}$

7. The fourth graders planted 1386 seeds on Earth Day in 2 hours. On average, how many seeds did they plant each hour?

______

8. The fifth graders cleaned up the park. They picked up 1071 pieces of trash in 3 hours. On average, how many pieces of trash did they pick up each hour?

______

Dividing by Multiples of 10

You know several ways to find a quotient.

Use base ten blocks and share on paper plates.

$20\overline{)80}$ = 4

Share 80 ones on 20 plates. There will be 4 on each plate.

Use base ten blocks and subtract groups of the same number.

$20\overline{)80}$ = 4

Think: How many groups of 20 can be taken from 80?

Use the multiplication table and the four steps DMS↓.

Look at the leading digits, 2 divided into 8 is 4.

$20\overline{)80}$

×	1	2	3	4	5	6	7	8	9
2	2	4	6	8	10	12	14	16	18

Find the quotients using base ten blocks.

1. $30\overline{)90}$ **2.** $50\overline{)100}$ **3.** $10\overline{)800}$ **4.** $90\overline{)180}$

5. $40\overline{)160}$ **6.** $30\overline{)2400}$ **7.** $80\overline{)6400}$ **8.** $60\overline{)4200}$

Solve.

9. For a city league, 270 kids were divided evenly onto 30 softball teams. How many kids were on each team? ________

10. Cotopaxti is a volcano in Ecuador. It has erupted 50 times in the last 400 years. If the same number of years passed between eruptions, how often would it have erupted? ________

11.  **What basic division fact will help you find the quotient of 1200 divided by 30? How many zeros will be in the quotient?**

TEST PREP

An auditorium holds a total of 800 people. There are 20 seats in each row. How many rows are there?

A 40
B 400
C 780
D 16,000

Ⓐ Ⓑ Ⓒ Ⓓ

Dividing by 2-Digit Numbers

There is $156 to be shared by 12 people. How much will each person get?

You can use base ten blocks to find the quotient.

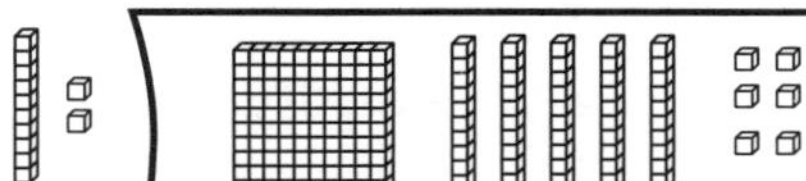

If 1 $100 bill, 5 $10 bills and 6 $1 bills are shared with 12, each will get 1 $10 bill and 3 $1 bills or $13.

Take apart equal groups on 12 paper plates.

Each plate will receive 1 ten and 3 ones or 13.

You can use DMS↓.

```
   013
12)156
   12
    36
    36
     0
```

$ ______

Use base ten blocks to find the quotient.

1\. ______

2\. ______

Use DMS↓ to find the quotient.

3. 21)462 **4.** 34)714 **5.** 22)682 **6.** 23)943

7. A clothing company divided 875 t-shirts evenly into 25 boxes for shipping. How many shirts were in each box? ______

8. Jake's mother made $828 last week. If she worked 36 hours, how much did she get paid each hour? ______

Problem-Solving Strategies

You can use different strategies to solve a problem.

A muffin pan holds 12 muffins. Sally baked 5 full pans. How many muffins did Sally bake?

Five Steps in Problem Solving

Step 1. Read and understand.
Step 2. Find the question and needed facts.
Step 3. Decide on a process.
Step 4. Estimate.
Step 5. Solve and check back.

Which strategy could I use to solve the problem?

I could...

1 ... act it out.
2 ... use a model.
3 ... draw a picture.
4 ... simplify.
5 ... make a table.

$12 \times 5 =$ _____ muffins

Read the problem. Identify which of the strategies (1–5 above) could be used to solve the problem. Follow the steps to answer the questions.

1. A hot dog vendor sold 4 trays of hot dogs. There were 18 hot dogs on each tray. How many hot dogs were sold?

Strategies?______________________

What is the process?______________

Estimate ________ Answer ________

2. John's uncle gave him 22 stamps which makes the total in his collection 378. How many stamps did John have originally?

Strategies?______________________

What is the process?______________

Estimate ________ Answer ________

3. Sue is going on a 10-day trip to Alaska. She plans to spend $85 a day for gas. How much will she spend for gas?

Strategies?______________________

What is the process?______________

Estimate ________ Answer ________

4. Sue bought 272 postcards on her trip. She used 8 postcards on each page of a scrapbook. How many pages did she fill?

Strategies?______________________

What is the process?______________

Estimate ________ Answer ________

5. Four vendors sold 15 hot dogs, 28 hot dogs, 41 hot dogs, and 39 hot dogs. How many hot dogs were sold in all?

Strategies?______________________

What is the process?______________

Estimate ________ Answer ________

6. A car averages 30 miles per gallon of gas. How many gallons will be needed to travel a distance of 150 miles?

Strategies?______________________

What is the process?______________

Estimate ________ Answer ________

$n = ?$

Maintaining the Balance

An equation is like a teeter-totter. Whatever is done on one side must also be done on the other side for the equation (the teeter-totter) to stay balanced.

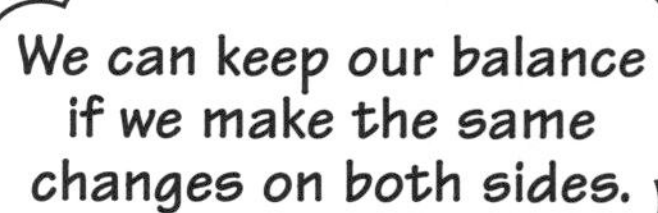

If I add 5 pounds to my side, you'll have to add 5 pounds to your side.

Tell if the balance scale shows a balanced or a not balanced equation.

1.

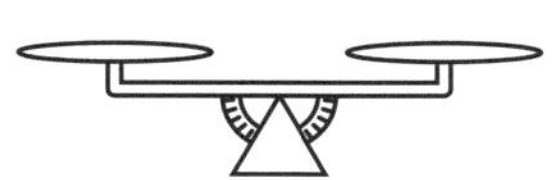

balanced not balanced

2.

balanced not balanced

The two ends of a teeter-totter are balanced. Describe what change must be made to the other side to keep the balance when ...

3. 5 pounds is added on the right side.

____

____

4. 10 grams is taken off the left side.

____

____

5. the weight on the left side is doubled.

____

____

6. 20 pounds is added on the right side.

____

____

Indicate what number goes in the box to keep a balanced equation.

7. $9 + 4 = 9 + \square$ **8.** $12 + 2 = 12 + \square$ **9.** $6 \times 2 = 6 \times \square$ **10.** $5 \times 3 = \square \times 3$

Look at the balance scale. If we add five pounds to both sides, what will happen? Explain your answer by using words, a picture, and an equation.

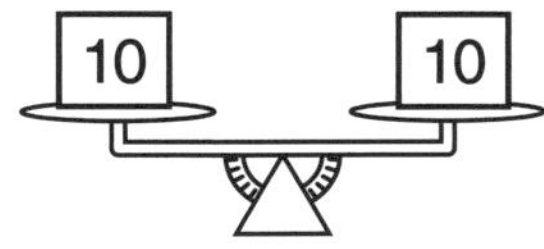

$n=?$

Maintaining a True Equation: The Properties of Equality

An equation is like a balance scale. Whatever is done to one side must be done to the other side for the scale to balance and the equation to be true. The properties of equality tell us how equations remain balanced.

Add the same number on both sides of an equation and the sides remain equal.

$5 + 2$ $5 + 2$

$7 = \square$

A

Multiply both sides of an equation by the same number and both sides remain equal.

5×2 5×2

$10 = \square$

B

Does scale C show an equation? ______
How do you know? ________________

2×6 $2 \times (3 + 3)$

$12 = \square$

C

Does scale D show an equation? ______
How do you know? ________________

5×4 $4 \times 2 + 5$

$20 > \square$

D

Do the balance scales show an equation? Show how you know.

1. 3×4 2×6

____

Yes or No

2. 6×3 2×8

____

Yes or No

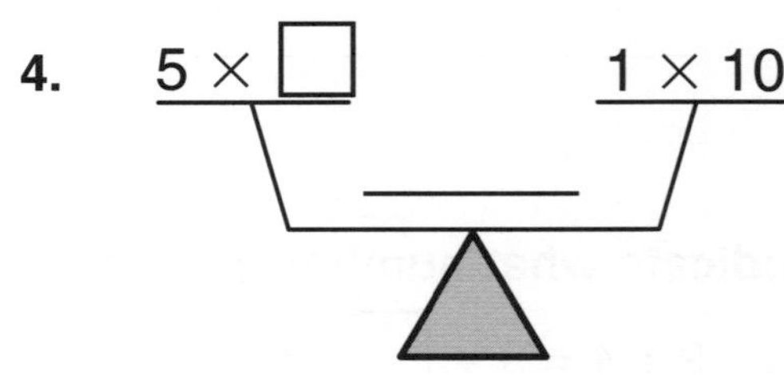

What number goes in the box to make the equation true?

3. $5 + 4$ $5 + \square$

____

4. $5 \times \square$ 1×10

____

What number will balance the scale?

5. $4 + (5 \times 2)$ $2 \times \square$

$\square =$ ______

6. $2 \times (10 + 4)$ $4 \times n$

$n =$ ______

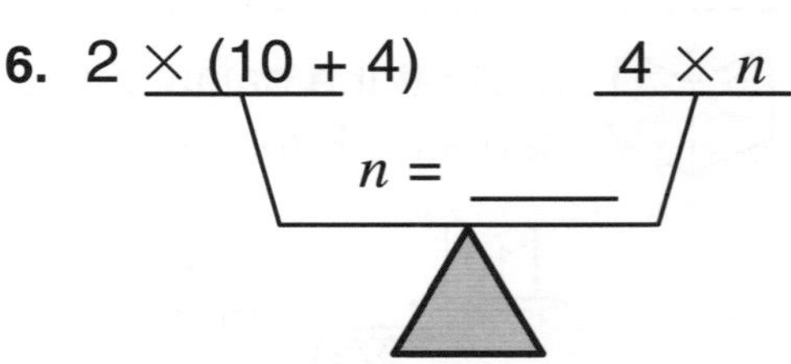

7. **What is an equation? What operations can you use on both sides of an equation to keep the equation equal?**

$n = ?$

Name ______________________ Score __________

Multiplication, Division, Problem-Solving Review

1. What is another way to write 3 + 3 + 3 + 3 + 3?

______ (Obj. 20)

A $3 + 4$
B $3 \times 3 \times 3 \times 3 \times 3$
C 5×3
D $15 \div 3$

2. $\begin{array}{r} 5 \\ \times\ 4 \\ \hline \end{array}$ $7 \times 8 =$

______, ______ (Obj. 20)

3. What number goes in the box to make the statement true?

$2 \times 6 = \square \times 2$

$\square =$ ______ (Obj. 20)

$3 \times (\square \times 5) = (3 \times 2) \times 5$

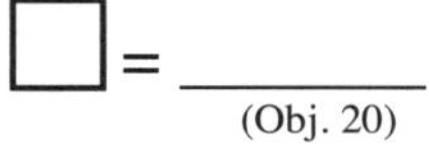

$\square =$ ______ (Obj. 20)

4. Write all the factors of 12.

______________________ (Obj. 25)

5. $\begin{array}{r} 13 \\ \times\ 5 \\ \hline \end{array}$ $\begin{array}{r} 172 \\ \times\ 4 \\ \hline \end{array}$

______, ______ (Obj. 21)

6. Choose the best estimate for $6 \times 37¢$.

______ (Obj. 21)

A $6 \times 20¢$
B $6 \times 30¢$
C $6 \times 40¢$
D $6 \times 50¢$

7. $\begin{array}{r} 10 \\ \times\ 40 \\ \hline \end{array}$ $80 \times 40 =$

______, ______ (Obj. 22)

8. $\begin{array}{r} 43 \\ \times\ 21 \\ \hline \end{array}$ $\begin{array}{r} 52 \\ \times\ 37 \\ \hline \end{array}$

______, ______ (Obj. 23)

9. There are 24 rows of chairs in the auditorium. There are 12 chairs in each row. How many chairs are there in all?

______ (Obj. 21)

10. Which is another way to write:

______ (Obj. 25)

$\begin{array}{r} 12 \\ -\ 4 \\ \hline 8 \end{array}$ $\begin{array}{r} 8 \\ -\ 4 \\ \hline 4 \end{array}$ $\begin{array}{r} 4 \\ -\ 4 \\ \hline 0 \end{array}$

A $12 - 4 = 8$
B $12 + 4 = 16$
C $12 \div 4 = 3$
D $12 \div 2 = 6$

11. $5\overline{)35}$ $72 \div 8 =$

______, ______ (Obj. 25)

12. Write two multiplication facts and two division facts for the array.

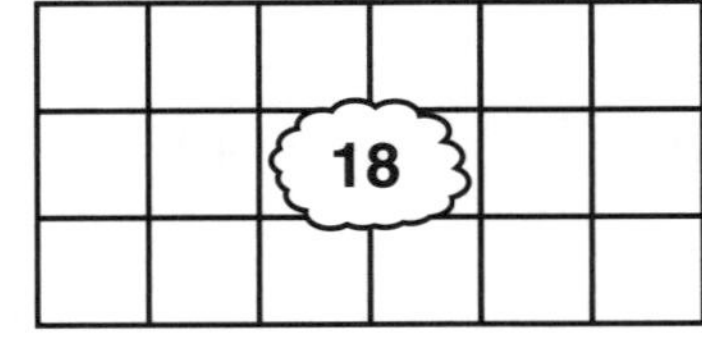

____________, ____________

____________, ____________ (Obj. 25)

13. A package of 6 snack crackers costs 48¢. What is the cost of one cracker?

________ (Obj. 26)

14. $3\overline{)96}$ $6\overline{)87}$

______, ______ (Obj. 26)

15. $5\overline{)275}$ $4\overline{)1746}$

______, ______ (Obj. 27)

16. $4\overline{)408}$ $3\overline{)6045}$

______, ______ (Obj. 28)

17. A bushel of 224 apples is split evenly into 7 baskets. There are the same number of apples in each basket. How many apples are in each basket?

________ (Obj. 26)

18. Phil's mother bought 6 packages of hamburger buns. There are 8 buns in each package. How many buns did she buy?

________ (Obj. 21)

19. There are 9 rows of seats in a theater. Each row has the same number of seats. If there are 162 seats in the theater, how many seats are there in each row?

________ (Obj. 26)

20. Write a number sentence for the words in the box.

The product of 2 and *n* is 6.

________________________ (Obj. 24)

21. What is the name of the answer in a division problem?

________ (Obj. 29)

A difference **C** sum
B product **D** quotient

22. Find the mean and the mode:

6, 9, 5, 4, 6

mean ________

mode ________

Name ____________________

Daily Review

1. Write the number 654 in expanded notation.

____

(Obj. 1)

2. Which set of numbers is in order from greatest to least? ______ (Obj. 2)

A 247, 265, 334, 374

B 374, 334, 247, 265

C 374, 334, 265, 247

D 365, 247, 265, 334

3. A number machine makes numbers from a rule. What number comes next? ______ (Obj. 3)

6, 12, 18 ____

4. What number is shown? ______ (Obj. 4)

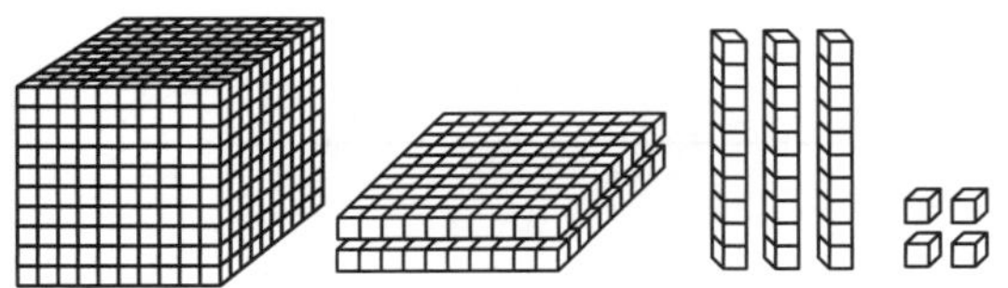

5. Write the words that name the number 15,200.

____

____

(Obj. 5)

Name ____________________

Daily Review

1. The population of New Town is 157,462. What digit is in the ten thousands place? ______ (Obj. 6)

2. What is the best estimate for 31 + 49? ______ (Obj. 7)

A 30 + 40   C 40 + 40

B 30 + 50   D 40 + 50

3. Which is another way to write 5 + 5 + 5? ______ (Obj. 20)

A $3 + 5$ C 3×5

B $5 \times 5 \times 5$ D $15 \div 5$

4. What multiplication fact is shown? ______ (Obj. 20)

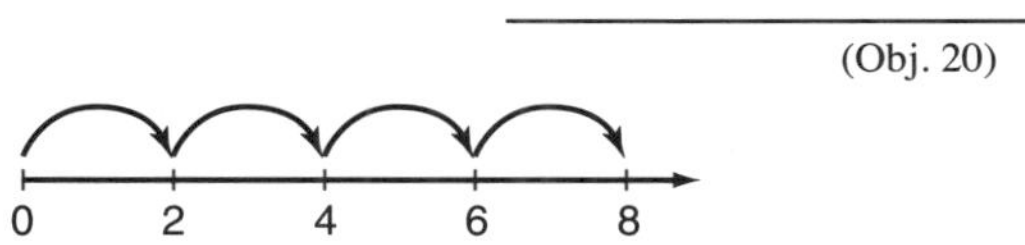

5. What number goes in the box to make a true statement? ______ (Obj. 20)

$5 \times \square = 5$

Name ______________________

1. The park had 3654 visitors. What is this number rounded to the nearest hundred?

______ (Obj. 8)

2. What multiplication fact is shown?

______ (Obj. 20)

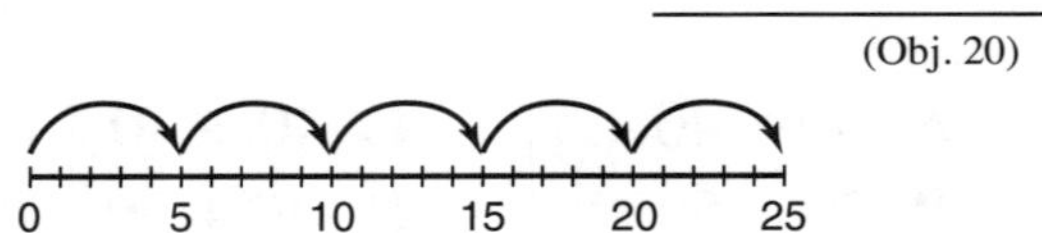

3. Which is another way to write $2 + 2 + 2 + 2 + 2$?

______ (Obj. 20)

A $10 \div 2$ **C** $3 + 5$
B 2×5 **D** $2 \times 2 \times 2 \times 2 \times 2$

4. What number goes in the box to make a true statement?

______ (Obj. 20)

$2 \times \square = 2$

5. What number goes in the box to make a true statement?

______ (Obj. 20)

$2 \times \square = 0$

Name ______________________

Daily Review

1. What number goes in the box to make a true statement?

______ (Obj. 9)

$(4 + 7) + 6 = 4 + (\square + 6)$

2. Write a multiplication fact for the array.

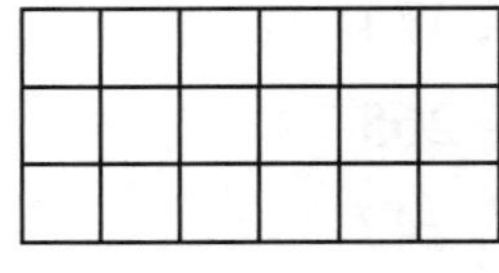

______ (Obj. 20)

3. What number goes in the box to make a true statement?

______ (Obj. 20)

$2 \times 6 = \square \times 2$

4. Write the multiples of 4.

(Obj. 20)

×	0	1	2	3	4	5	6
4							

5. Write the multiples of 3.

(Obj. 20)

×	0	1	2	3	4	5	6
3							

Name ____________________________

Check 1 Point

1. Which is another way to write $3 + 3 + 3 + 3$? ________ (Obj. 20)

   A $3 + 4$
   B $3 \times 3 \times 3 \times 3$
   C $12 \div 3$
   D 3×4

2. What multiplication fact is shown? ________ (Obj. 20)

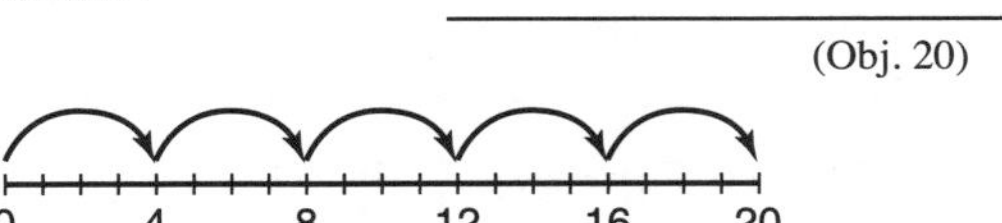

3. What number goes in the box to make the number sentence true? ________ (Obj. 20)

   $\square \times 6 = 0$

4. Write a multiplication fact for the array. ________ (Obj. 20)

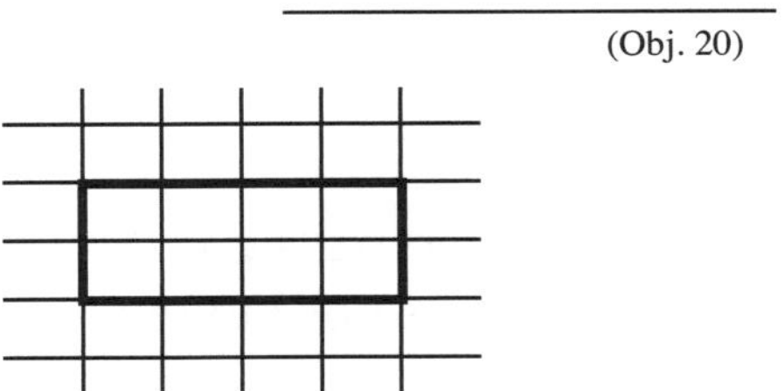

5. Multiply. ________ (Obj. 20)

   $3 \times 4 = \square$

6. Write the multiples of 5. (Obj. 20)

×	0	1	2	3	4	5
5						

7. What number goes in the box to make the number sentence true? ________ (Obj. 20)

   $2 \times 4 = \square \times 2$

8. $6 \times 7 =$ ________ (Obj. 20)

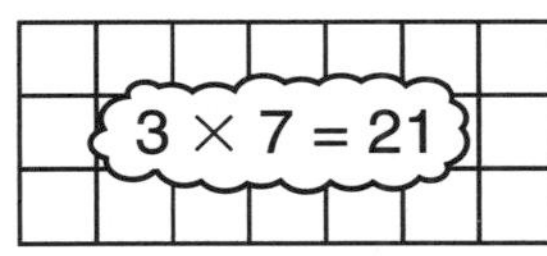

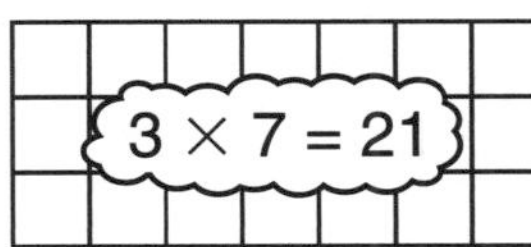

9. $\begin{array}{r} 7 \\ \times\ 8 \\ \hline \end{array}$ $8 \times 9 =$ ________, ________ (Obj. 20)

10. You have 3 pairs of shoes. How many shoes do you have? Draw a picture. Write a number sentence. ________ (Obj. 20)

Name ____________________

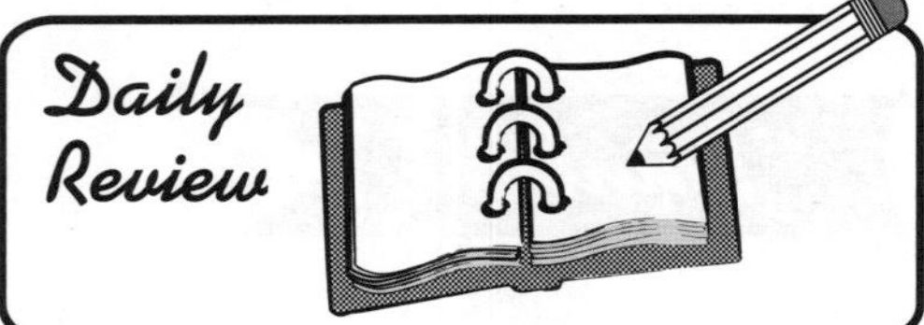

1. $\begin{array}{r} 698 \\ +\ 250 \\ \hline \end{array}$

______ (Obj. 10)

2. $\begin{array}{r} 3 \\ \times\ 9 \\ \hline \end{array}$ $9 \times 8 =$ ______, ______ (Obj. 20)

3. $\begin{array}{r} 10 \\ \times\ 7 \\ \hline \end{array}$ $8 \times 10 =$ ______, ______ (Obj. 20)

4.

$3 \times 3 =$

______ (Obj. 20)

5. Complete the table of multiples. (Obj. 20)

×	0	1	2	3	4	5
8						

×	6	7	8	9	10
8					

Review 6

Name ____________________

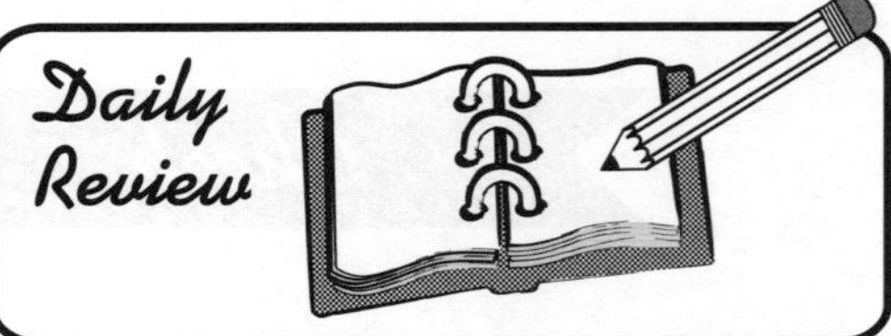

1. $\begin{array}{r} 53 \\ 34 \\ +\ 56 \\ \hline \end{array}$

______ (Obj. 11)

2. What number goes in the box?

______ (Obj. 20)

No. of Hands	1	2	3
No. of Fingers	5	10	

3. $\begin{array}{r} 4 \\ \times 9 \\ \hline \end{array}$ $9 \times 9 =$ ______, ______ (Obj. 20)

4. What number goes in the box to make the number sentence true?

$3 \times (2 \times 5) = (3 \times \square) \times 5$

______ (Obj. 20)

5. Playground balls cost $6 each. Find the cost of buying 2 to 5 balls. (Obj. 20)

No. of Balls	1	2	3	4	5
Total Cost	$6				

Review 7

Name ______________________

Daily Review

1. Ben's father drove 2367 miles in August and 1375 miles in September. How many miles did he drive in August and September?

______ (Obj. 12)

2. $\begin{array}{r} 30 \\ \times\ 4 \\ \hline \end{array}$ $3 \times 40 =$ ______, ______ (Obj. 22)

3. You earn $20 a week for helping with chores. How much do you earn in 4 weeks?

______ (Obj. 22)

4. Complete the multiplication.

$\begin{array}{r} 12 \\ \times\ 4 \\ \hline \end{array} = \begin{array}{r} 10 + 2 \\ \times\ 4 \\ \hline \end{array}$

______ + ______ = ______ (Obj. 21)

5. $\begin{array}{r} \$21 \\ \times\ 4 \\ \hline \end{array}$ $\begin{array}{r} \$34 \\ \times\ 2 \\ \hline \end{array}$ ______, ______ (Obj. 21)

Name ______________________

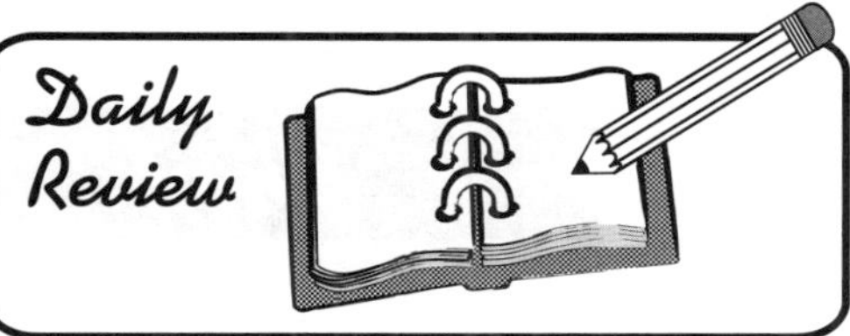

1. The table shows the number of students in each grade.

Grade	No. of Students
2	117
3	120
4	95

How many students are in the three grades combined?

______ (Obj. 13)

2. Write a multiplication fact for the array.

______ × ______ = ______ (Obj. 20)

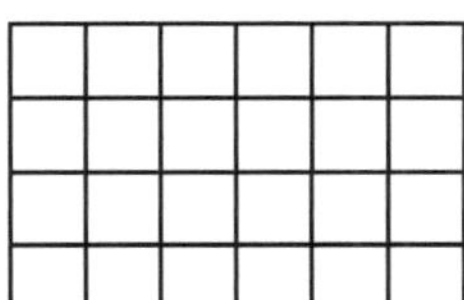

3. $\begin{array}{r} 14 \\ \times\ 4 \\ \hline \end{array}$

______ (Obj. 21)

4. There are 36 caramels in a bag. How many caramels are in 2 bags?

______ (Obj. 21)

5. $\begin{array}{r} 46 \\ \times\ 5 \\ \hline \end{array}$

______ (Obj. 21)

Name ______________________

Check 2 Point

1. $\begin{array}{r} 9 \\ \times 7 \\ \hline \end{array}$ $8 \times 9 =$ ______, ______ (Obj. 20)

2. List the squares of each number from 2 to 9. (Obj. 20)

square ______ ______ ______ ______
(2) (3) (4) (5)

square ______ ______ ______ ______
(6) (7) (8) (9)

3. What number goes in the box?

Number of Feet	1	2	3	4
Number of Toes	5	10	15	☐

______ (Obj. 20)

4. What number goes in the box to make the number sentence true?

$(3 \times 2) \times \square = 3 \times (2 \times 4)$

______ (Obj. 20)

5. $\begin{array}{r} 50 \\ \times 3 \\ \hline \end{array}$

______ (Obj. 22)

6. $\begin{array}{r} 34 \\ \times 2 \\ \hline \end{array}$

______ (Obj. 22)

7. $\begin{array}{r} 16 \\ \times 4 \\ \hline \end{array}$

______ (Obj. 22)

8. Estimate the product by rounding the 2-digit number to the nearest 10.

$5 \times 48 =$ ____ $\times$ ____ $=$ ______ est. (Obj. 20)

9. Estimate the product by rounding the cents to the nearest 10¢.

$4 \times 21¢ =$ ____ $\times$ ____¢ $=$ ______¢ est. (Obj. 20)

10. Mrs. Swanson made 18 costumes for the class play. Each costume took 4 yards of material. **About** how many yards of material did she need for all of the costumes?

______ (Obj. 25)

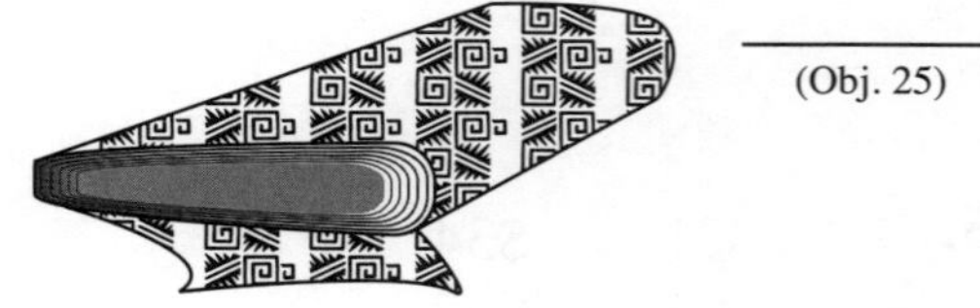

Name ____________________

Daily Review

1. Write the number sentence for the words in the box.

The sum of 12 and 5 is n.

______________________ (Obj. 14)

2. $\begin{array}{r} 36 \\ \times\ 5 \\ \hline \end{array}$

______ (Obj. 21)

3. $\begin{array}{r} 212 \\ \times\ 4 \\ \hline \end{array}$

______ (Obj. 21)

4. $\begin{array}{r} 162 \\ \times\ 3 \\ \hline \end{array}$

______ (Obj. 21)

5. There are 180 days in a school year. How many days are there in 3 school years?

______ (Obj. 21)

Name ____________________

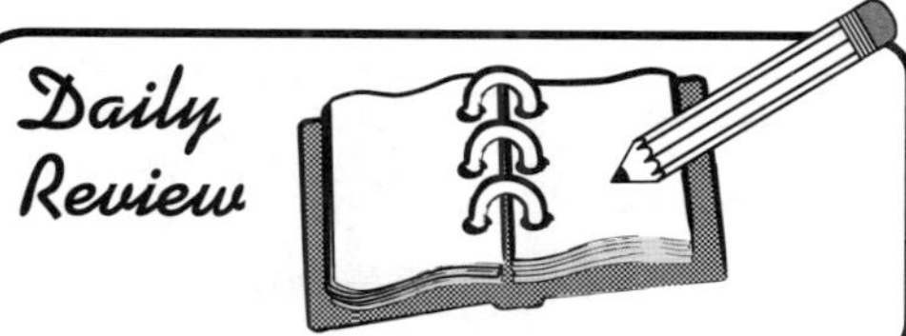

1. $\begin{array}{r} 318 \\ -\ 146 \\ \hline \end{array}$

______ (Obj. 15)

2. $\begin{array}{r} 37 \\ \times\ 6 \\ \hline \end{array}$

______ (Obj. 21)

3. $\begin{array}{r} 304 \\ \times\ 2 \\ \hline \end{array}$

______ (Obj. 21)

4. $50 \times 10 =$

______ (Obj. 22)

5. Amy's average reading rate is 203 words per minute. How many words can she read in 5 minutes?

______ (Obj. 21)

Name ______________________________

Daily Review

1. There are 205 students in the third grade. There are 188 students in the fourth grade. How many more students are there in third grade?

________ (Obj. 16)

2. $30 \times 40 =$ ________ (Obj. 22)

3.
$$\begin{array}{r} 12 \\ \times\ 13 \\ \hline \end{array}$$

________ (Obj. 23)

4.
$$\begin{array}{r} 23 \\ \times\ 18 \\ \hline \end{array}$$

________ (Obj. 23)

5. Estimate the product by rounding each number to the nearest ten and then multiplying:

$$\begin{array}{r} 52 \\ \times\ 37 \\ \hline \end{array}$$

Est. ___ × ___ = ______

Actual ______ Reasonable? (yes or no)

(Obj. 23)

Name ______________________________

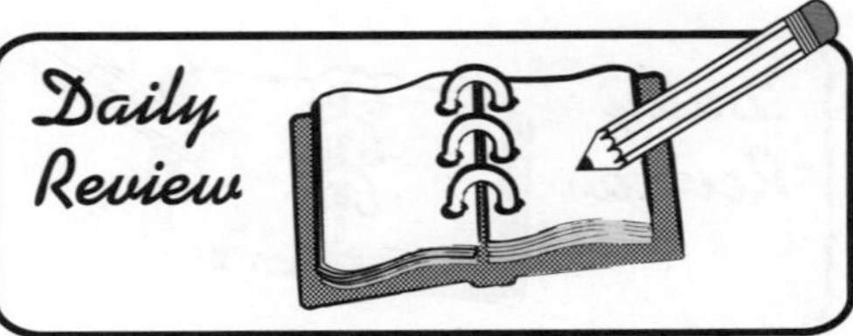

1.

POPULATION	
Jamestown	67,429
Ft. Pierce	24,674
Castle Rock	7,321

The table shows the population of 3 cities. How many more people live in Jamestown than Ft. Pierce?

________ (Obj. 17)

2. Estimate the product of 68×41.

Est. ___ × ___ = ______ (Obj. 23)

3. A merchant sold 83 radios for $23 each. How much did he earn from selling the radios?

________ (Obj. 23)

4. **Write a number sentence with parentheses to solve this problem:** You buy 2 sodas for 60¢ each and pay with a $5.00 bill. How much change (c) should you get?

number sentence: ____________________ (Obj. 47)

$c =$ ______

5. List all of the factors of 6.

Factors: ____________________ (Obj. 25)

Name ______________________

Check 3 Point

1. $\begin{array}{r} 157 \\ \times\ 6 \\ \hline \end{array}$

______ (Obj. 21)

2. $\begin{array}{r} 403 \\ \times\ 2 \\ \hline \end{array}$

______ (Obj. 21)

3. $20 \times 80 =$

______ (Obj. 22)

4. Each of the 24 baseball teams has 25 players. How many players are on the baseball teams in all?

______ (Obj. 23)

5. Estimate the product by rounding each number to the nearest ten.

72×49

Est. ______________________ (Obj. 23)

6. Write a number sentence using parentheses to solve the problem. You buy 2 notebooks for 39¢ each and pay with a $5.00 bill. How much change (c) should you receive?

number sentence: ______________ (Obj. 47)

$c =$ ______

7. Which number is prime?

4, 6, 7, 8

______ (Obj. 25)

8. How many different rectangles can you make with 8 squares?

______

The number 8 (is, is not) prime (Obj. 25)

9. Write one expression for the phrase. Use n for the number.

The product of 3 and a number.

______ (Obj. 24)

10. Use the letter n to write a number sentence for the words in the box below. Solve for n.

Product of 4 and a number is 28.

____

$n =$ ______ (Obj. 24)

Name ____________________

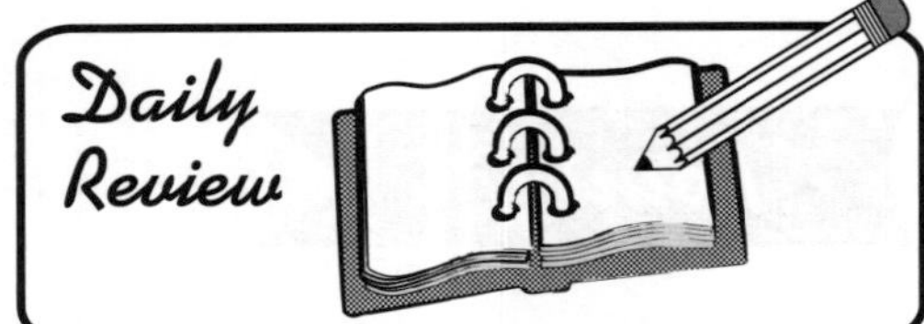

1. $7896 - 62 =$

(Obj. 18)

2. 312×3

(Obj. 21)

3. 25×43

(Obj. 23)

4. Two friends share 10 cards. How many cards will each friend receive?

(Obj. 25)

5. Circle groups of 2.
How many groups are there?

(Obj. 25)

○○○○○
○○○○○

Name ____________________

Daily Review

1. Write the number sentence for the words in the box.

(Obj. 19)

The difference of 14 and 5 is *n*.

2. A farmer has 39 rows of orange trees. There are 26 trees in each row. How many trees in all?

(Obj. 23)

3. Write a division fact for each multiplication fact. (Obj. 25)

$2 \times 4 = 8$ $5 \times 3 = 15$

4. $5\overline{)5}$ $3 \div 1 =$

______, ______
(Obj. 25)

5. $0 \div 4$ $2\overline{)0} =$

______, ______
(Obj. 25)

Name ____________________

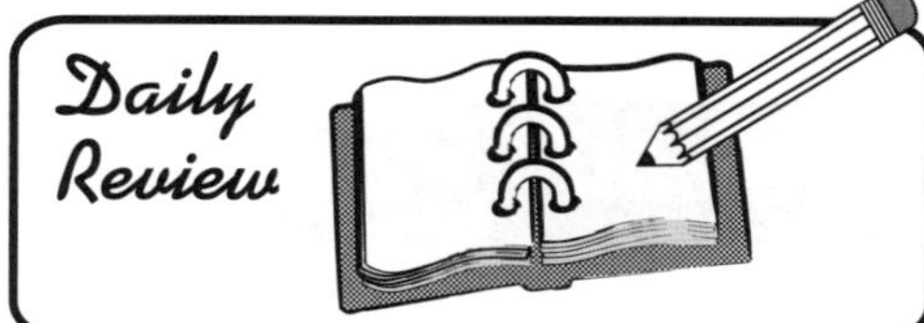

1. You bought a book for \$2.85. You paid the clerk with a \$5.00 bill. How much money will you have left?

______ (Obj. 47)

2. Circle groups of 3. How many groups are there?

______ (Obj. 25)

○○○○○○
○○○○○○

3. What division fact is shown?

______ (Obj. 25)

$$\begin{array}{r} 15 \\ -3 \\ \hline 12 \end{array} \quad \begin{array}{r} 12 \\ -3 \\ \hline 9 \end{array} \quad \begin{array}{r} 9 \\ -3 \\ \hline 6 \end{array} \quad \begin{array}{r} 6 \\ -3 \\ \hline 3 \end{array} \quad \begin{array}{r} 3 \\ -3 \\ \hline 0 \end{array}$$

4. How many 2-foot ribbons can be cut from a 12-foot spool?

______ (Obj. 25)

5. Write a family of 4 facts related to the numbers 3, 9, and 27.

______, ______

______, ______ (Obj. 25)

Review 18

Name ____________________

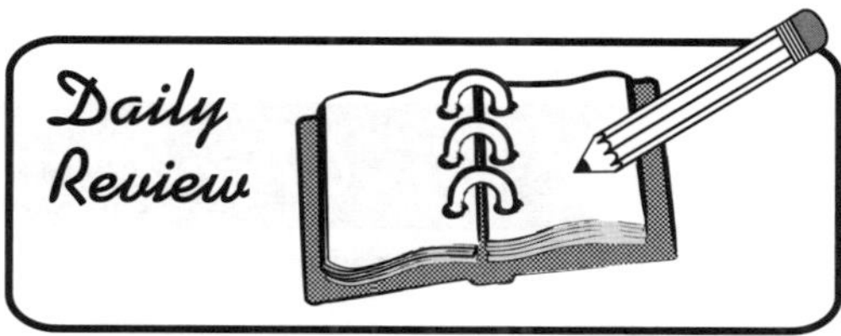

1. What are the coordinates of point P?

______ (Obj. 48)

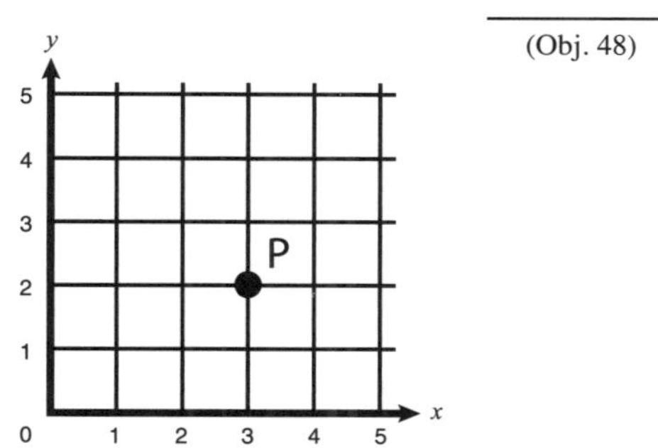

2. Write a family of 4 facts related to the numbers 4, 8, and 32.

______, ______

______, ______ (Obj. 25)

3. $4\overline{)28}$ $18 \div 3 =$ ______, ______ (Obj. 25)

4. Think of how many units are on the missing side. Write the division fact in 2 ways.

______, ______ (Obj. 25)

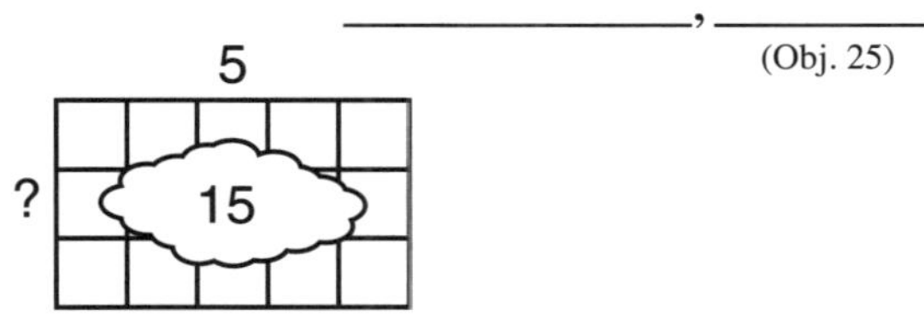

5. A package of 3 crackers costs 18¢. Find the cost of one cracker.

______ (Obj. 26)

Review 19

Name ______________________

Check 4 Point

1. There are 12 children on the playground. They are divided equally into 2 teams. How many children are on each team?

______ (Obj. 25)

2. Circle groups of 5. How many groups of 5 are there?

______ (Obj. 25)

3. What division fact is shown?

______ (Obj. 25)

$$\begin{array}{r} 15 \\ -5 \\ \hline 10 \end{array} \quad \begin{array}{r} 10 \\ -5 \\ \hline 5 \end{array} \quad \begin{array}{r} 5 \\ -5 \\ \hline 0 \end{array}$$

4. Write a family of 4 facts related to the numbers 5, 7, and 35.

______, ______

______, ______ (Obj. 25)

5. $4\overline{)28}$ $\quad 24 \div 3 =$ ______, ______ (Obj. 25)

6. Think of how many units are on the missing side. Write the division fact in 2 ways.

______, ______ (Obj. 25)

6

? 18

7. A package of cheese slices costs 45¢. There are 5 slices in a package. How much does 1 slice of cheese cost?

______ (Obj. 26)

8. Share equally. How many are in each basket?

______ (Obj. 25)

9. $28 \div 7 \quad 7\overline{)56} =$ ______, ______ (Obj. 25)

10. $48 \div 6 \quad 6\overline{)42} =$ ______, ______ (Obj. 25)

Name ____________________

Daily Review

Use the chart to answer questions 1 and 2.

Student	No. Books Read
Jan	
Kim	
Dan	
Tom	
	Each means 5 books

1. How many more books did Tom read than Kim? ______ (Obj. 50)

2. How many books did Dan and Jan read altogether? ______ (Obj. 50)

3. Write a division fact and a multiplication fact for the array.

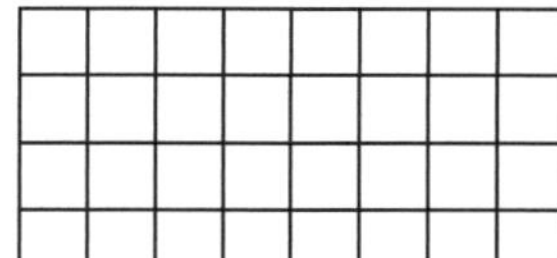

multiplication fact: ____________________

division fact: ____________________ (Obj. 25)

4. $8\overline{)56}$ $72 \div 9 =$

______, ______ (Obj. 25)

5. $63 \div 9 =$ $8 \times \square = 48$

______, ______ (Obj. 25)

Review 21

Name ____________________

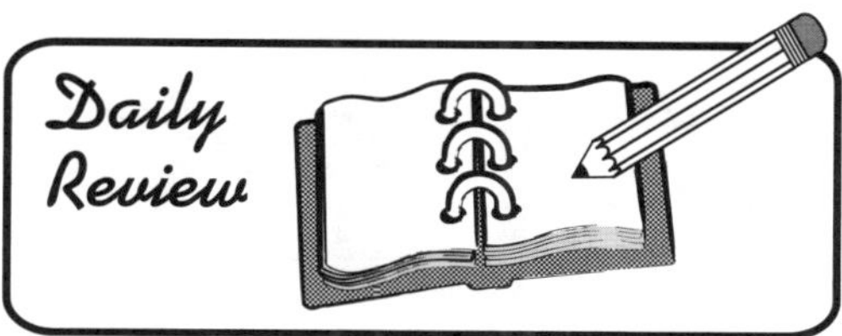

1. Peggy bought a soda for $0.89. She gave the cashier a $5.00 bill. **About** how much money will she have left?

______ (Obj. 47)

2. Chris bought a bag of cookies for $0.75 and a pie for $2.35. She gave the cashier a $5.00 bill. **About** how much change should she receive?

______ (Obj. 47)

3. $6\overline{)14}$ R

______ (Obj. 26)

4. Six bagels fit in a bag. How many bags will you need for 26 bagels?

______ (Obj. 26)

5. Each shelf is 3 feet long. How many shelves can you cut from a 10-foot board?

______ (Obj. 26)

Review 22

Name ____________________

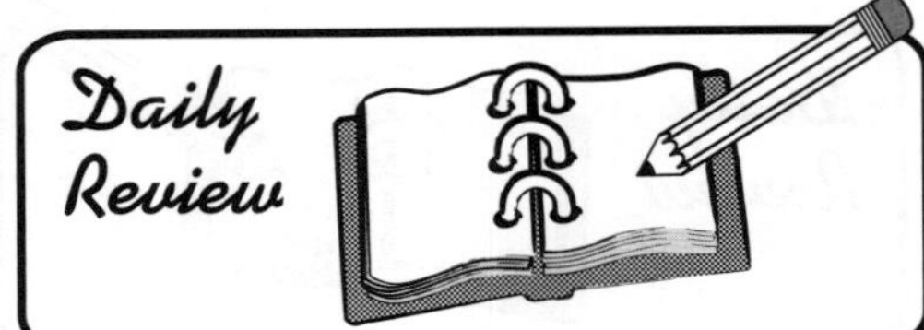

1. Write a division fact for the array.

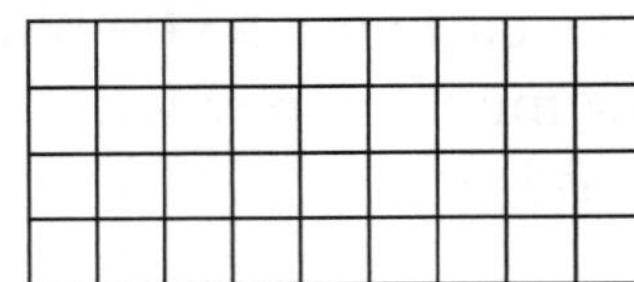

division fact: ____________________

(Obj. 25)

2. Six pencils fit in each box. You have 40 pencils. How many boxes will you need?

______

(Obj. 26)

3. $3\overline{)96}$

______

(Obj. 26)

4. $4\overline{)84}$

______

(Obj. 26)

5. There were 63 tennis balls. Three balls were put in each can. How many cans were filled?

______

(Obj. 26)

Name ____________________

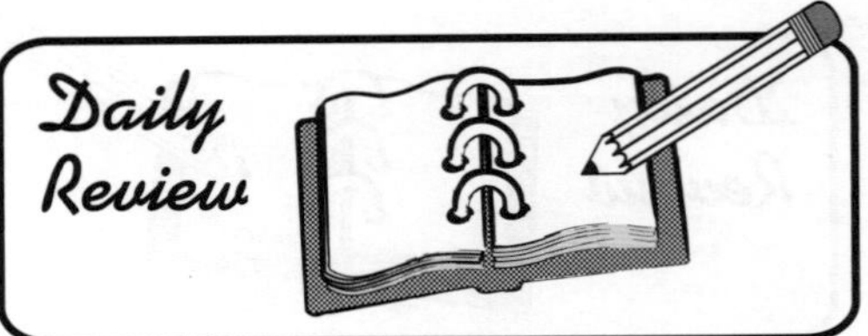

1. $4\overline{)88}$

______

(Obj. 26)

2. $3\overline{)69}$

______

(Obj. 26)

3. $5\overline{)75}$

______

(Obj. 26)

4. If you can jump rope 72 times in 3 minutes, how many times can you jump in 1 minute?

______

(Obj. 26)

5. $3\overline{)34}$ **R**

______

(Obj. 26)

Name ______________________

Check 5 Point

1. $8\overline{)64}$ $72 \div 9 =$

______, ______
(Obj. 25)

2. $7\overline{)30}$ R

______
(Obj. 26)

3. Each table seats 6 students. How many tables are needed to seat 26 students?

______
(Obj. 26)

4. $4\overline{)84}$

______
(Obj. 26)

5. $3\overline{)93}$

______
(Obj. 26)

6. $8\overline{)96}$

______
(Obj. 26)

7. $3\overline{)85}$ R

______
(Obj. 26)

8. Jan got scores of 6, 9, 8, and 5 on her Checkpoint quizzes. What is Jan's mean score?

______
(Obj. 50)

Use the temperature data below to answer questions 9 and 10.

The low temperatures for five days were:

50° 38° 42° 50° 44°

9. Find the mode temperature.

______
(Obj. 50)

10. Find the median temperature.

______
(Obj. 50)

Name ______________________

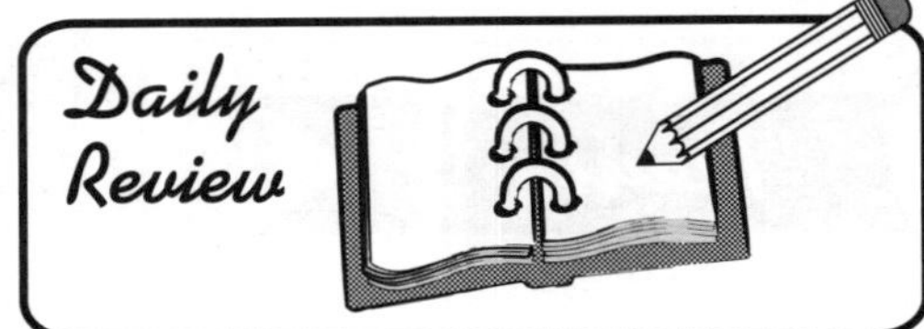

1. Which symbol goes in each box? (Obj. 29)

3 ☐ 6 = 18   21 ☐ 3 = 7

2. Which would give you the quotient for 12 and 4? ______ (Obj. 29)

A 12 + 4   **C** 12 × 4
B 12 – 4   **D** 12 ÷ 4

3. $3\overline{)639}$ ______ (Obj. 27)

4. $4\overline{)392}$ ______ (Obj. 27)

5. Cort needs to read a book in 5 days. If the book has 180 pages, how many pages should he read each day? ______ (Obj. 27)

Review 26

Name ______________________

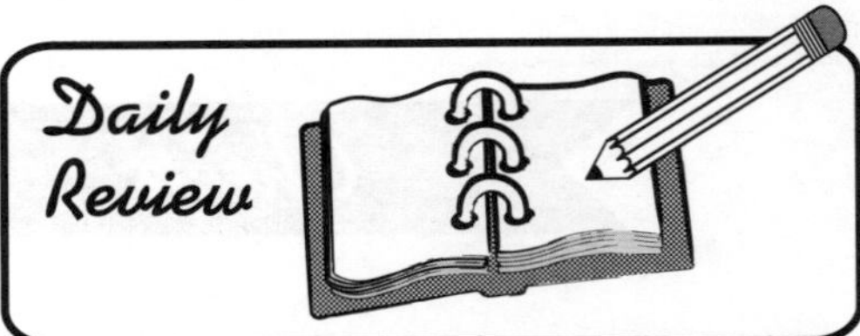

1. $5\overline{)535}$ ______ (Obj. 27)

2. $7\overline{)9184}$ ______ (Obj. 27)

3. $80\overline{)6400}$ ______ (Obj. 28)

4. $12\overline{)276}$ ______ (Obj. 28)

5. What number goes in the box to balance the scale? ______ (Obj. 29)

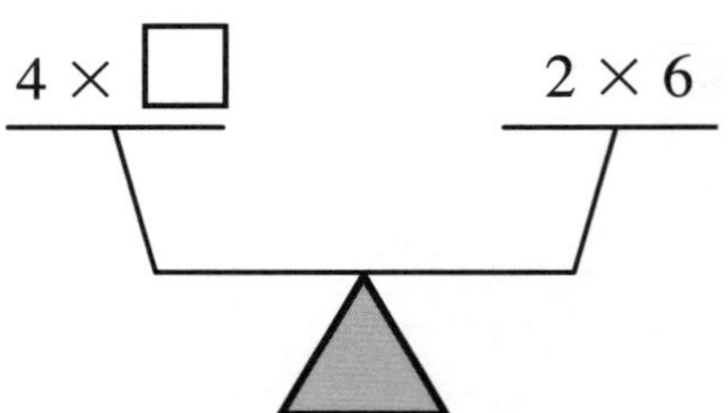

Review 27